Sociology of
Education

Jill Swale

**Advanced
Topic*Master***

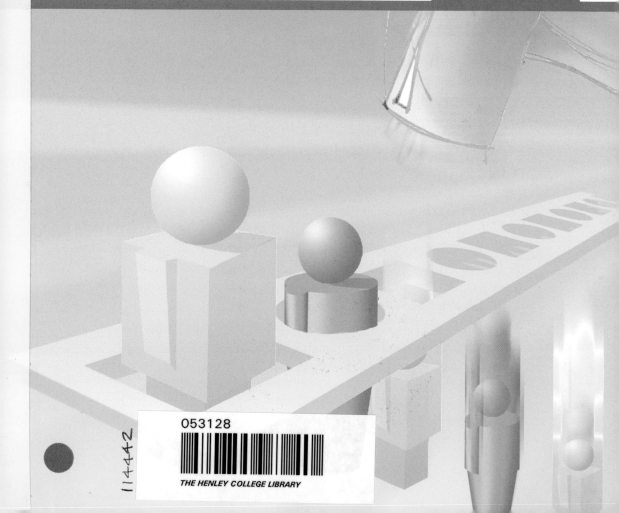

Philip Allan Updates
Market Place
Deddington
Oxfordshire
OX15 0SE

Orders
Bookpoint Ltd, 130 Milton Park, Abingdon, Oxfordshire, OX14 4SB
tel: 01235 827720
fax: 01235 400454
e-mail: uk.orders@bookpoint.co.uk
Lines are open 9.00 a.m.–5.00 p.m., Monday to Saturday, with a 24-hour message
answering service. You can also order through the Philip Allan Updates website:
www.philipallan.co.uk

ISBN: 978-1-84489-632-5

Printed in Spain

Philip Allan Updates' policy is to use papers that are natural, renewable and
recyclable products and made from wood grown in sustainable forests. The
logging and manufacturing processes are expected to conform to the environmental regulations of the country of origin.

Contents

7 How does education relate to global problems?

Introduction

For most people, education is a major influence on how they conduct the rest of their lives. It can lead to a stimulating career and an affluent lifestyle or to disillusionment, unemployment or even a life of crime. On a national level, an education system might produce an efficient workforce or a generation of independent thinkers and caring, informed citizens. Alternatively, schools can reinforce bigotry, as in Germany under Hitler and in South Africa under apartheid. Education is, therefore, a fascinating area of sociological interest.

Chapter 1 compares different views of education, examining whether education divides society or acts as a unifying force and whether it needs radical change.

Chapters 2, 3 and 4 focus on the varying attainment levels of particular groups, exploring alternative explanations as to why these occur. The under-achievement of some working-class and ethnic-minority students is explored further in Chapter 5, with greater emphasis on processes within schools, such as labelling by teachers, streaming and the formation of subcultures.

Chapter 6 examines education policies and legislation from 1870 to 2006, focusing on themes such as equal opportunities, vocationalism, raising standards and education as a competitive marketplace. Chapter 7 provides a stark reminder that millions of the world's children have little or no education at all. It concludes with a consideration of how British education might increase awareness of the plight of the world's poor and issues relating to equality and the environment.

While reading the chapters in numerical order is recommended, there is a glossary to enable you to look up explanations that you may have bypassed.

A major aim of this book is to bring the sociology of education to life. Hence Chapters 2 to 5 contain relatively brief summaries of influential early studies followed by more detailed accounts of recent research, complete with lively quotations from interviews with students and teachers and from classroom observations. I hope students will find these highly memorable. I have included more detail about how the studies were conducted than appears in other textbooks, because this makes it easier to evaluate the research and, therefore, to pick up extra marks in essays. The examples can also be used when writing about methods for other units.

I hope you enjoy reading about Paul Dixon, Spanksy, the Real Englishmen and the Posse!

Jill Swale

What are the roles of the education system?

Functionalist views of education

What is education for? If someone asked why you are studying your present courses, you would almost certainly answer in terms of your personal goals and interests. You are probably studying sociology because you need A-levels to get into university or to obtain a better job and, hopefully, because you find the subject intriguing. These motives all relate to you as an individual. However, some sociologists have a very different way of answering similar questions. In fact, sociologists disagree strongly among themselves about what education is for and even whether it is good for people! This chapter will explore some of their disagreements.

Structuralists are sociologists who view aspects of social life, such as education, in terms of how they affect whole groups of people and institutions in society. They are more interested in how education affects the economy and stability of the country than in which subjects students find the most fulfilling. Not all researchers are macrosociologists, interested in studying large social systems. Microsociologists are much more interested in how people react to, and influence each other in, small groups — for example, in classrooms.

Emile Durkheim: school as a socialising agent

Emile Durkheim (1858–1917), one of the founding fathers of sociology, was a particular type of structuralist known as a functionalist. He took the conservative view that all the institutions of society exist because they have useful functions, contributing to the general good. This perspective meant that he was not very critical of institutions such as education, the family and religion because he was focusing on what they achieved in ideal circumstances. Many sociologists, including Marxists and liberals, strongly disagree with his views. Nevertheless, he made interesting points about the functions of education.

In 1902–03, Durkheim gave a series of lectures at the Sorbonne in Paris, later published as the book *Moral Education: A Study of the Theory and Application of the Sociology of Education*. According to Durkheim, as every individual has to coexist with other people, one of the main purposes of education should be to socialise children into the norms and values agreed by society — the **value consensus**. Instead of following their own impulses, children must learn self-restraint, fit in with the patterns of behaviour adopted by others and accept the discipline imposed by the school.

> To act morally is to act in terms of the collective interest.

Durkheim's priority was an orderly and cohesive society. He acknowledged that social inequalities exist but viewed them as inevitable. Some students would be more academically successful than others and become wealthier, but all had their roles to play. It was better for many people to accept their limits and to contribute as far as possible to the general good, through fairly lowly roles. If everyone pursued their own personal progress obsessively and unrealistically it would lead to frustration, alienation and deviance, to the detriment of social order. Unrestricted freedoms are found only in anarchic societies, whereas 'through the practice of moral rules we develop the capacity to govern and regulate ourselves, which is the whole reality of liberty'.

Emile Durkheim

Visual Arts Library (London)/Alamy

Box 1.1

Extracts from Durkheim's *Moral Education*

Without trying to hide the injustices of the world — injustices that always exist — we must make the child appreciate that he cannot rely for happiness on unlimited power, knowledge or wealth, but that it can be found in very diverse situations…that the most important thing is to discover a goal compatible with one's abilities, one which allows him to realise his nature without seeking to surpass it in some manner, thrusting it violently and artificially beyond its natural limits. There is a whole set of mental attitudes that the school should help the child acquire…because they are sound and will have the most fortunate influence on the general welfare.

Durkheim stressed that the chief role of education should be to encourage in children a sense of **social solidarity**, a feeling of identification with the group and responsibility towards others. This was particularly important in modern industrialised societies, where rapid changes were thrusting people from many different backgrounds together.

In his opinion:

- increasing rates of crime were signs of egoism — people pursuing their own goals rather than the good of the community
- higher levels of suicide were symptomatic of anomie — a lack of shared values and a feeling of moral confusion
- education had an essential binding role to play in societies in which religion was becoming less influential

Teaching social solidarity through school subjects

Of course, learning about academic subjects and vocational skills was essential too, especially as developments in technology meant that more specialists in different fields were required and fewer people learned traditional trades from their families. Many school subjects could also be used to demonstrate messages about people's interdependence.

The study of cells in biology could provide an illustration of the child's role in society:

> We have here inorganic elements which, in combination and association, suddenly manifest completely new properties characterizing life. Here is one thing that will make the child understand…that in one sense a whole is not identical with the sum of its parts. This can lead him on the road to understanding that society is not simply the sum of individuals that compose it.
>
> E. Durkheim, *Moral Education* (1925)

Teaching history should not emphasise the achievements of a few exceptional individuals, but raise awareness of how progress has been achieved by the cooperation of previous generations. Children need to appreciate society's cultural traditions so that they become an integral part of it.

> It is, therefore, this collective consciousness that we must instil in the child.

Are Durkheim's views relevant nowadays?

In 2001, riots in the north of England were partially blamed on the education system. The disturbances arose as a result of tensions within the divided communities in Bradford, Oldham and Burnley. These tensions were made worse because the residents lived in areas segregated along ethnic lines, with students of different origins attending different schools. According to the Ouseley Report on the situation in Bradford, the city's schools had done little to promote understanding between ethnic groups.

Since 2001, the government has been less eager to encourage faith schools, because the children who attend them may be less likely to feel social solidarity with those of different backgrounds.

Bradford riots

David Hargreaves: applying Durkheim's views to comprehensive schools

Writing much more recently, David Hargreaves has broadly endorsed Durkheim's view that education should promote solidarity. However, in *The Challenge for the Comprehensive School* (1982) he regrets that a sense of community is more often lacking in modern schools than in Durkheim's day. Though some students are highly motivated and a few are deliberately disruptive, Hargreaves is more alarmed by two larger groups, which he claims comprise the majority of comprehensive school pupils:

- 'Instrumental' students are those who work without enthusiasm for either the subjects or the school and merely to gain qualifications that they know they need. They are influenced by what Durkheim terms egoism, a negative form of individualism that has been encouraged by the competitive atmosphere of the school.
- 'Indifferent' students scarcely work at all. They are bored, but too passive to cause real trouble. These students display anomie — a lack of commitment that is likely to continue throughout their adult lives.

The existence of these two large groups of students indicates that the social solidarity advocated by Durkheim is becoming harder to attain.

Hargreaves suggests several reasons why this has occurred. Comprehensive schools are usually large and often cater for students' varying abilities by teaching them in different groups for different subjects. They are unlikely to spend much time together as a form — a potential source of community identity. He describes 'the Luton airport effect' at the end of every lesson.

> The children stream round the building, but are now armed with huge cases…in which all their possessions are kept. There is no corporate home, no collective responsibility and yet teachers are puzzled that there is no institutional pride.
>
> D. Hargreaves, *The Challenge of the Comprehensive School* (1982)

The decline of house systems and whole school assemblies contributes to the lack of community spirit in schools.

Hargreaves has modified Durkheim's ideas, suggesting that students need to experience a sense of belonging not just to the whole school community but to a variety of communities. In this way, they will learn to manage the conflicting demands of different groups. Some of his suggestions are shown in Box 1.2.

Box 1.2

Ways to foster group solidarity in schools

According to Hargreaves, ways to foster group solidarity include:

- cooperative group projects within the classroom
- community studies, including community service
- school plays
- school camps
- inter-school sports
- house activities and competitions

How relevant are Hargreaves's ideas today?

Independent learning is currently promoted in schools, but Hargreaves warns of its dangers.

> It is good that pupils should not be too dependent upon their teachers, but a collection of autonomous and self-reliant individuals does not and cannot produce a community.

Hargreaves is probably right that we should expect schools to integrate people from diverse backgrounds. After the London bombings of 2005, the public were startled to hear that the suicide bombers had been brought up in Britain and even more astonished that one had taught in a school here.

Task 1.1

Suggest three reasons why the teaching of the subject of citizenship in schools since 2002 may fulfil the requirements of an effective education as recommended by Durkheim and Hargreaves.

Guidance

Try to make links between:

- learning about UK laws and political systems
- community service and group activities, such as school councils
- tolerating opposing views in discussions

and

- collective consciousness
- social solidarity
- self-restraint in the interests of others

Citizenship projects, such as this one involving the emergency services, may foster group solidarity

Talcott Parsons: school as a bridge

The USA is a 'melting pot' society made up of people from different national origins and religions, so it is unsurprising that American functionalists have supported Durkheim's views about the socialising roles of schools. Talcott Parsons, writing in the 1950s, viewed school as a bridge between home and work, as outlined below:

Home

In the family, the child is judged by particularistic standards and is valued as a son or daughter, rather than according to skills displayed. The parents may behave in ways different from the national norms. These factors range from major differences, such as speaking another language, to minor traits, such as having special family words for particular things.

School — a bridge between home and the workplace

School provides a halfway house. It enables the child to master the national language, to fit into the unnatural rhythms of a large community (e.g. by only eating at specified times) and to learn the value consensus. Idiosyncrasies tolerated at home are likely to drop away. Yet the school is a less harsh environment than the workplace, with teachers acting *in loco parentis*. Allowances are made for small children and there is a fair amount of play in the early years.

Workplace

In the workplace, employees are assessed by universalistic standards relating to skill, and by conformity to rules, including punctuality and deference. They may be sacked if they do not comply. If people successfully negotiate the change from the relatively undemanding environment of the home to the more competitive place of employment, they can gain achieved status that is unrelated to their family background

According to functionalists, all children are treated equally at school and are expected to work and to follow rules. The system is a meritocracy in which those who develop their skills and work hard are rewarded accordingly, regardless of social background. Rewards come in the form of qualifications and appropriate role allocation. Students will eventually be selected for jobs according to the skills they have developed at school and the qualifications they have gained. In large industrialised societies, there have to be objective measures by which employers can quickly assess the suitability of potential candidates for jobs. These measures are provided by the examination system. Most people accept this as a fair system.

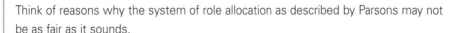

Task 1.2

Think of reasons why the system of role allocation as described by Parsons may not be as fair as it sounds.

Guidance

- Some sociologists do not believe that schools are meritocracies.
- There is evidence that social background results in students being treated differently. Working-class and some ethnic-minority students may be assigned to lower streams and achieve inferior qualifications.
- Social background and identity may also affect role allocation. Discrimination prevents some people from gaining employment that is appropriate to their qualifications.

Davis and Moore: justifying inequality

Inevitably, while most well-qualified students obtain top jobs and good salaries, less successful school-leavers take humdrum work with low wages. Functionalists regard this as a necessary aspect of a competitive and free society. Kingsley Davis and Wilbert Moore, American sociologists contemporary with Parsons, argued that high wages are necessary to attract competition for the roles most functionally important to society. Who would bother with doctors' long medical training and responsibilities if they were only paid the same as office assistants?

By sifting students according to ability, awarding varying qualifications and encouraging the gifted to specialise, the education system provides the employees required by the economy at all levels. Functionalists regard this as a necessary and fair system. In contrast, Marxists take a critical stance, focusing on the masses of children destined for drudgery. They argue that schools generate inequality and mass poverty.

Marxist views of education

Like functionalists, Marxists are structuralists or macrosociologists — they take an overview of society, but through much more critical eyes than functionalists. To understand their views of schools, it is helpful to be reminded of the origins of Marxism.

Karl Marx (1818–83) was concerned by the inequalities between the social classes in Western societies in the mid-nineteenth century:

- A very small proportion of wealthy people owned huge amounts of land and factories, i.e. the means of production. These were the bourgeoisie, also known as the ruling class or capitalists.
- Most of the population worked for the bourgeoisie as waged labourers. These members of the proletariat were exploited, receiving only just enough money to survive. They had no control over the work process and no share in the profits. As society became industrialised and more competitive, it was likely that these workers would become increasingly alienated because they worked on production lines in the detailed division of labour, repeating a few mindless repetitive tasks without seeing the final product.

Why did workers accept this dull and impoverished life? According to Marx, the economic base of capitalism was reinforced by a superstructure of institutions such as religion, government, the family and education, which taught people to accept their lot in life.

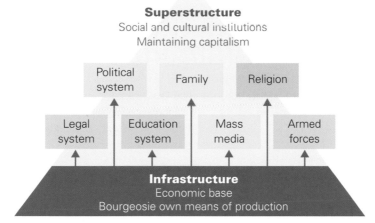

Figure 1.1 Marxist model of a capitalist system

There were enough workers to start a revolution and create a communist state in which ordinary people could take over the means of production and share profits fairly. However, this was unlikely to happen because the proletariat existed in a state of false consciousness. They accepted inequalities as inevitable, often regarding themselves as not clever or worthy enough to deserve better. Capitalist ideology, a set of biased beliefs, taught them that the powerful members of society deserved respect and that the contemporary hierarchy was blessed by God. In addition, they were struggling so hard to survive that they regarded other workers as competitors rather than allies. Hence, they lacked the working class solidarity needed to oppose the bourgeoisie effectively.

Marx was describing western capitalist societies a century-and-a-half ago, but modern Marxists believe his ideas to be still broadly true. Britain is not as sharply divided between social classes as in Marx's time, but harsh inequalities remain. Marxists focus on the potential for struggle between the proletariat asserting their rights and the bourgeoisie trying to hold on to power. Therefore, the Marxist view is known as a conflict perspective. In contrast, functionalism, with its stress on shared values and the benefits to all of keeping society orderly and united, is known as a consensus perspective. Modern followers of Marx agree with his view that the education system is one of the main agents of control, depriving working-class children of opportunities to improve their economic situation.

Bowles and Gintis: the correspondence principle

Samuel Bowles and Herbert Gintis's Marxist study *Schooling in Capitalist America* (1976) is still considered an important text today. The writers felt that education should be a means of social mobility. They were disappointed that efforts to

help working-class students through compensatory education projects in the 1960s seemed to have little effect and were soon abandoned.

> Since World War 1, there has been a dramatic increase in the general level of education in the United States, as well as a considerable equalization of its distribution among individuals. Yet economic mobility — i.e. the degree to which economic success (income or occupational status) is independent of family background of individuals — has not changed measurably. And the total effect of family background on educational attainment (years of schooling) has remained substantially constant.
>
> S. Bowles and H. Gintis, Schooling in Capitalist America (1976)

They did not accept that the lower achievements of generations of poorer children were due to low inherited IQ. Through statistical analysis of a large sample of white males, they found that educational attainment was strongly dependent on social background, even for students of similar childhood IQs. This affected the number of years spent in education and the quality of the college courses chosen.

Bowles and Gintis claimed that schools were organised to prepare most students to become docile manual workers, willing to work for the profit of capitalists. Most were repressed. Only a small minority were encouraged to be independent and ambitious original thinkers, and these tended to be middle- and upper-class students destined to be professionals and leaders of capitalist organisations.

> Thus in high school, vocational and general tracks emphasise rule-following and close supervision, while the college track tends toward a more open atmosphere emphasizing the internalization of norms.
>
> S. Bowles and H. Gintis, Schooling in Capitalist America (1976)

One of their research methods was to ask high-school students to rate each other on personality traits shown at school. These ratings were then compared with school records of student grades. Those students rated as creative, aggressive and independent were penalised by the school with lower grades than students who were punctual, dependable and tactful. Thus, initiative was discouraged among students who were likely to leave school at the minimum age.

> Somewhat higher up the educational ladder, teacher and community colleges allow for more independent activity and less overall supervision. At the top, the elite four-year colleges emphasise social relationships conformable with the higher levels in the production hierarchy.
>
> S. Bowles and H. Gintis, Schooling in Capitalist America (1976)

This process — passing a set of attitudes and behaviour patterns on to students through the school's **hidden curriculum** — explained why working-class children rarely entered higher professions. According to Bowles and Gintis, unlike the official curriculum of subjects taught, the hidden curriculum of a school consisted of:

- the values transmitted unofficially through the ways teachers treated different groups of students
- hierarchies within the staff
- how the school was organised
- the formal and informal rewards and punishments
- underlying messages in teaching materials, such as textbooks, about the achievements of upper-class white males

Bowles and Gintis's correspondence principle is so-called because it illustrates parallels between school and work conditions. Marxists believe that the education system is organised to prepare students for future roles in a capitalist system in which working-class children will form the proletariat, with the higher classes dominating as the bourgeoisie.

Task 1.3

Read the passage and think about the question below.

> Schools foster legitimate inequality through the ostensibly meritocratic manner by which they reward and promote students and allocate them to distinct positions in the occupational hierarchy.
>
> S. Bowles and H. Gintis, *Schooling in Capitalist America* (1976)

Consider what Bowles and Gintis say about the 'ostensibly meritocratic manner' in which some children are rewarded and promoted in schools, for example by gaining high marks, being promoted to higher streams, sitting challenging examinations and acquiring the qualifications needed for good jobs.

Check what functionalists mean by meritocracy. Why do functionalists accept meritocracy as fair and necessary, while Marxists question its validity?

Guidance

- The marks given for assignments and teachers' decisions whether to allocate students to a top examination set might be influenced by assumptions about their motivation and the working-class peer group to which they belong.
- We are used to accepting that some students will perform poorly at school ('inequality').
- If some students do better than others at school, this will seem 'legitimate'. Those who fail are likely to assume that it is because they are not clever enough and consequently they will accept unrewarding jobs.

Some correspondences between the social relationships of school and of the workplace are shown in Table 1.1.

Table 1.1	Correspondences between the social relationships of school and the workplace	

School	Workplace
Students get used to hierarchies such as head teacher, head of department, teacher, teaching assistant. Deference is required; students might address male teachers as 'Sir'.	Companies have hierarchies of managers and assistant managers, who must be respected.
Students have no school territory where they can escape from adult supervision, whereas teachers have staff rooms that students cannot enter. Teachers may have more comfortable chairs. Students are likely to have to wear uniforms, unlike teachers.	Bosses have better offices than workers and do not wear overalls.
Students are expected to obey without question. Free expression is penalised.	Shop-floor workers must follow instructions. Alternative approaches are unpopular.
School provides extrinsic rewards (qualifications at the end of the process), rather than intrinsic rewards (interesting lessons and choice). Lessons may involve dull exercises and worksheets.	Factory work is dull and repetitive. Only the wages make it worthwhile.
Schoolwork is fragmented into different subjects. At the changeover of lessons, students have to break off from unfinished tasks.	Tasks are fragmented on a production line so workers rarely have the satisfaction of making a whole object.
Ordinary high schools supervise students and impose many rules. Students at elite colleges are trusted to behave well.	Shop floor workers are closely supervised, whereas bosses and professionals are simply expected to act responsibly.
Schools take a register and punish lateness and time wasting, whereas elite colleges may operate on trust.	Workers often have to clock in and lose pay if they are late. Bosses work flexible hours.

If most young people are destined for manual or low-skilled office jobs, why is compulsory education so long? Two reasons given are:

- It takes time to get children used to accepting boredom and doing as they are told.
- It helps capitalists to have more skilled workers than there are suitable jobs available.

Those who fail to find employment form a reserve army of labour — people desperate enough to accept low wages. Their existence is a reminder to workers that if they demand higher wages they can easily be replaced.

Marxists are also interested in how privileged young people learn to become bourgeoisie. In Britain, public schools foster leadership through systems of prefects, heads of house and armed forces cadet schemes. The schools often occupy former ancestral homes in extensive grounds.

In state schools, the minority who stay on to the sixth form are prepared for their roles as professionals by receiving additional privileges such as their own common rooms. They may become prefects, supervising other students.

Support for Bowles and Gintis

Marxist Louis Althusser (1969)

Althusser commented that ordinary people would not accept unequal work conditions and pay unless something convinced them that it was inevitable. In the past, religion taught that suffering brought rewards. Nowadays, the education system teaches people to accept their situation. People learn to accept Western capitalism, with little positive information about communism or other alternatives.

Students are taught that they fail or succeed according to their own efforts and talents. They do not realise that they may be being held back by streaming and teacher labelling based partly on their social background. Examinations are designed to fail a proportion of candidates and governments are reluctant to create enough good jobs.

Marxist Paulo Freire (1970)

The USA withdrew funding from a primary education programme in Brazil because they feared its radical ideas would tempt new generations into revolution. The educationalist responsible for the programme, Paulo Freire, viewed the main purpose of schooling not as training for employment but as a way of encouraging critical thinking — teaching peasants to examine and challenge their exploitation by landowners. In *Pedagogy of Freedom* (1970) he wrote that the teacher's role should be to help students to question and change society. He was imprisoned for his beliefs. Capitalists viewed his type of education as worse than leaving the poor in ignorance.

Questioning Bowles and Gintis

Marxist Paul Willis (1977)

For his study *Learning to Labour: How Working Class Kids Get Working Class Jobs*, Willis observed and interviewed 12 working-class boys towards the end of their schooling and in their early months in factory work. He found the opposite of docility in these students. They realised that their backgrounds destined them for unskilled work, so they studied as little as possible, livening up the time by being cheeky to teachers and mocking hardworking students (known as ear'oles).

Their fatalistic attitudes resulted from a realistic assessment of their class position, passed on from parents in working-class jobs. Their academic failure arose from the anti-school subculture they formed, not from the hidden curriculum. In the factory, they passed the time joking around to alleviate boredom.

Willis's study was still Marxist, because it recognised the influence of class inequalities and identified correspondence between the lads' attitudes to school and to work. However, they were not in a state of false consciousness, fooled by the ideology of fairness and meritocracy. Rather than directly opposing the system through political activity, they made the best of it by 'having a laff'.

Are Bowles and Gintis's views relevant to modern British schools?

Points supporting the relevance of Bowles and Gintis's views include the following:

- There are major differences between the school experiences and likely destinies of students taught in public schools and those of students in the lower streams of comprehensives.
- There are clear signs of hierarchy in UK schools — for example, there are different toilets, furniture and personal space for students and staff at different levels.

Points against the relevance of Bowles and Gintis's views include the following:

- Schools now pay at least lip-service to thinking skills and independent learning.
- Students at many secondary schools have opportunities to influence the running of the school through school councils. Citizenship encourages democratic decision making.
- Subjects such as sociology and critical thinking encourage students to question ideologies and assumptions.
- The pressure of league tables and OFSTED inspections encourages schools to seek good academic results from students of all backgrounds.

Liberal views of education

We have noted that functionalists and Marxists are structuralists. Although they disagree strongly about the fairness of the education system, both groups focus on how situations in schools affect the economy, power relationships and stability of the whole nation. Liberal sociologists are still interested in these issues, but they stress the need for education to teach people to think independently, to take part in democratic processes and to fulfil themselves through leisure interests. While Marxists view people as members of two conflicting classes and prioritise a more equal society, liberals focus on the well-being of individuals and, as their name suggests, on freedom from having to conform to the demands of any group.

John Dewey, who wrote *Democracy and Education* in 1916, stressed the need to 'liberate and direct energies' of individual children, channelling their varying interests to help them grow mentally, spiritually, emotionally and physically into well-rounded and independent human beings. Learning should proceed through direct observation and experiments rather than through rote learning and routines that have the effect of 'rendering the work of both teacher and pupil mechanical and slavish'. Factual knowledge can quickly become out of date, so fostering initiative and the desire to learn is more important.

> All that the school can or need do for pupils, so far as their minds are concerned...is to develop their ability to think.

In order to cope in a mobile and democratic society, children need to be able to communicate tolerantly with people from different backgrounds, think independently and have the confidence and motivation to 'secure social changes without introducing disorder'. This is more feasible through a progressive educational system in which students are encouraged to solve problems individually instead of the teacher telling the whole class all the answers.

Some educators have pursued these ideals by setting up their own progressive schools. Summerhill, founded by A. S. Neill in 1924, had optional lessons and a school parliament to decide on school rules, in which students and teachers had equal voting rights. The rationale was that students would be more motivated to work on subjects they had chosen freely and would respond to the democratic regime by developing into responsible adults. Summerhill was, therefore, run along lines that contrast dramatically with the American high school conditions observed by Bowles and Gintis.

Task 1.4

Which of Dewey's ideas are influential today?

Guidance

Consider:

- science experiments
- problem-solving events
- teaching students according to different learning styles and multiple intelligences
- how often you explore ideas in groups and how often teachers 'spoon-feed' you

Deschooling society

Ivan Illich was another liberal thinker. He was so concerned about the way schools create passive recipients of knowledge that in *Deschooling Society* (1971) he suggested abolishing the school system. Students are 'mugs' to be filled up with facts from the teacher's 'jug'. This information is rarely needed, fully understood or enjoyed but it provides work for teachers and helps the government by making students conformist.

> School is the advertising agency which makes you believe that you need the society as it is.

Illich's belief was that people who learn what they want when they choose to do so are usually far more successful and can often manage without a highly qualified teacher. Illich suggested replacing the school system with other forms of learning to be available at any age, though the greatest uptake would probably be by the young. Students would be issued with education vouchers entitling them to the services of pedagogues — guides who could judge their levels of proficiency and suggest the best materials or experts to help them. Those who really wanted to learn a practical skill, such as cookery or a language, could learn it more effectively from a practising cook or native speaker

Ivan Illich

Time Life Pictures/Getty Images

than from a school teacher. Students interested in exploring more abstract subjects could advertise for matched peers to work with via a computer system. This would be run by network administrators employed to make the system work flexibly. Learning aids such as tools, laboratory equipment, books, artworks, educational games, printing presses and photographic equipment would be easily accessible to people of all ages and incomes, through libraries, museums and workplaces.

These schemes combined would break up the present power structure that imposes values and attitudes on the young and makes a poor job of teaching them the subjects prescribed by the official curriculum.

Are there problems with Illich's ideas?

Problems with these ideas include the following:

- How would children too young to work be occupied all day without schools?
- Who would ensure that they learned basic literacy, numeracy and social skills?
- How would students know what they would like to explore without exposure to it?
- Optional learning might be chosen predominantly by those with well-educated parents who appreciate the value of learning. This would increase the current social divide.

However, Illich's work is useful for the following reasons:

- It reminds us that students can learn for themselves by making independent use of resources.
- It makes us question school curricula. Are there really subjects that all students should learn? Could it be that specifications are designed by powerful people who want their own group to retain control?

Which views are most relevant today?

All the perspectives above are influential today:

- In a multicultural society, schools are expected to help children to integrate and cooperate, as functionalists such as Durkheim claimed.
- Many sociologists would agree with Bowles and Gintis that education has failed to close the attainment gap between the social classes, although more working-class children now study at A-level.
- Liberal views are reflected in personalised learning policies, group activities, choice in coursework topics and attempts to treat students as individuals through profiling and mentoring.

However, despite initiatives such as Every Child Matters, many lessons are still dominated by teacher-talk and large schools may resemble factories with learning fragmented by bells.

Summary

- Structuralists (macrosociologists) are interested in the functions of the education system for society — for example, how it prepares children to conform and contribute to the economy.
- Functionalists see one of the main roles of schools as passing on value consensus to children.
- Durkheim and Hargreaves stressed the need for education to encourage social solidarity, particularly in heterogeneous societies.
- Parsons viewed school as a bridge between the home and the workplace. Along with Davis and Moore, he regarded education as meritocratic. Schools award qualifications according to students' efforts and abilities, resulting in role allocation for employment.
- Marxists are structuralists who take a conflict view of society. The bourgeoisie exploit the proletariat, using the education system to perpetuate their ideology.
- Bowles and Gintis described the correspondence principle, demonstrating how schools prepared the proletariat for the passive drudgery of the workplace.
- Willis found anti-school subcultures that opposed authority, but he agreed that students' working-class origins led to working-class futures.
- Liberals Dewey and Illich changed the focus from mass education as a means of maintaining a social system to more flexible arrangements to meet the varying needs and interests of thinking individuals.

Task 1.5

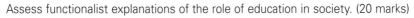

Assess functionalist explanations of the role of education in society. (20 marks)

Guidance

This typical AQA 20-mark essay question requires a range of skills. You need to:
- show breadth of knowledge and understanding by referring to several functionalists and their theories
- build in assessment, which means evaluating the theories; this is essential to earn high marks

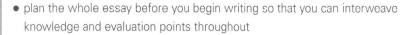
Task 1.5 (continued)

- plan the whole essay before you begin writing so that you can interweave knowledge and evaluation points throughout

First, explain the functionalist idea that the different institutions in society need to cooperate like parts of a body. Incorporate the following:
- Durkheim — norms and values, social solidarity
- Parsons — education system as a bridge, role allocation, meritocracy

Evaluation includes showing both agreement and disagreement between sociologists:
- Davis and Moore — agreement with Parsons on the fairness of role allocation
- Hargreaves — Durkheim's ideas are still applicable today, but less optimism about solidarity in schools

Sometimes you can assess particular studies by evaluating the methods used:
- Hargreaves's views are convincing because they are based on observation and teaching in schools.

You can question a study's relevance to modern Britain or point out a news event (e.g. the Bradford riots) that illustrates it.

Having assessed the functionalists 'from within', evaluate their work from other perspectives:
- Marxists :
  - Bowles and Gintis — schools not meritocratic; capitalist values and solidarity prevent the proletariat from asserting their rights
  - Willis — schools fail to promote the proletariat
- Liberals — Dewey and Illich stressed individualism more than the functionalists did

When introducing different perspectives, focus *only* on what they say about the role of education. Keep your essay relevant by explicitly comparing them with functionalist views.

Now write a substantial conclusion, summing up your assessment of the strengths and weaknesses of functionalist views on the role of education. This will earn more evaluation marks.

Research suggestions

- To what extent is there social solidarity in modern schools? Interview students and staff, preferably at several schools, to gauge whether there is any sense of group loyalty. If so, is it found more in forms, houses, teams or citizenship activities? You will need to consider how you will identify and measure 'group loyalty'.

- Interview teachers who have taught at faith schools and at schools with students from different religious backgrounds. Try to find out their views on how well such students integrate with the wider community. Your questions might be extended to students and parents, but a sensitive approach would be needed.
- Apply Bowles and Gintis's correspondence theory to one or more schools to assess how relevant it is to education in the UK today.

Useful websites

- Ruth's Sociology Resources — click on education
  www.mortonmail.com
- Dave Harris and Colleagues: Essays, Papers and Courses: Bowles and Gintis
  www.arasite.org/nbg2.htm
- Sociology at Hewett: education
  www.hewett.norfolk.sch.uk/curric/soc/EDUCATIO/edindex.htm

Further reading

- Illich, I. (1971) *Deschooling Society*, Calder and Boyars.
- Willis, P. (1977) *Learning to Labour: How Working Class Kids Get Working Class Jobs*, Saxon House.

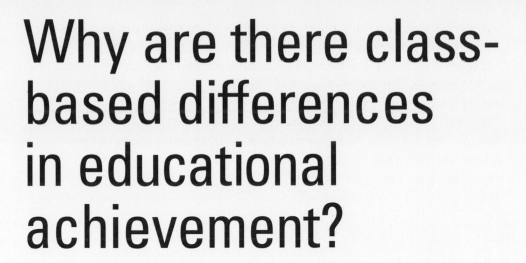

Why are there class-based differences in educational achievement?

Why are social-class differences in attainment important?

Sociologists have long been concerned by the unequal educational attainments of different social groups, particularly children of different social classes, ethnicities and sexes. If certain strata fail to reach their potential at school, this is likely to reduce their chances of full-time employment and limit the careers open to them. Hence, their earning power and entire lifestyle, and also those of their families, will be affected. Their contribution to society, likelihood of committing crime, mental and physical health, longevity and the educational achievements of their own children are all likely to be influenced by how well they do at school.

Figure 2.1 shows the attainment of five or more GCSE grades A* to C in England and Wales in 2002, by parental social class.

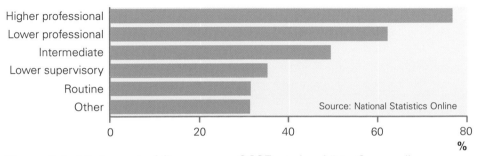

Figure 2.1 Attainment of five or more GCSE grades A* to C according to parents' social class, 2002, England and Wales

Figure 2.1 shows how dramatically students' GCSE results vary with the social class of their parents. In 2002, 77% of children in year 11 in England and Wales with parents in higher professional occupations gained five or more GCSEs at A* to C grades. This was more than double the proportion for children with parents in routine occupations (32%). Higher professionals include managers in large firms, doctors and lawyers; such people may be described as upper middle class. The term 'routine occupations' refers to unskilled manual jobs, such as factory work and cleaning. These are also known as lower working-class jobs. The educational attainment gap between children in these two groups, often contrasted briefly as 'middle class' and 'working class', is frequently studied by sociologists. (Another way that is often used to distinguish children of different social backgrounds is entitlement to free school meals.)

There has been more social mobility among intermediate workers — people working in such services as insurance, banking and travel agencies. Changes in the type of work available in postwar Britain have meant that many workers in today's service industry have parents who were manual workers. The children of intermediate workers are more likely to be upwardly mobile than the children of routine workers, so they are of less concern to sociologists.

It is possible to take or retake qualifications at a later age, and many people do so through the Open University and other institutions. However, good GCSE results are the usual gateway to A-levels and higher education. Some people successfully climb up the hierarchy of companies or set up their own businesses, but entry at degree level is more likely to result in a good income.

If education is almost vital to success, it is important that everyone should have equal access, opportunity and encouragement. This is not the case — only a minority of parents can afford private education. Even within state schools there are major differences in achievement between classes. Although intelligence tests indicate slight differences between middle-class and working-class people, in reality there is a great deal of overlap and the gap is too small to account for the wide differences in achievement.

Task 2.1

Before reading on, jot down several reasons why working-class children might perform less well at school. Add to your list as you go through the chapter and do wider research.

Guidance

Consider the following:

- home factors — income, attitudes and family traditions
- school factors — relationships with teachers, peer influence and school curriculum

As will be discussed in Chapter 6, social democrats campaigned for the selective education system to be replaced by comprehensive schools, to enable children of all social classes to receive education of a similar standard. Since 1965, working-class children have achieved more exam passes, but they are still outperformed by the middle classes, who are more likely to stay on at school. Ten times more children of professionals enter higher education than children of unskilled manual workers. Sociologists disagree about the main reasons for these class differences.

Are attainment differences due to material factors?

In *Education Divides: Poverty and Schooling in the 1990s* (1995), Teresa Smith and Michael Noble identify several barriers to learning that are related to income. Problems experienced by poorer children include:
- insufficient money to purchase uniforms or to participate in activities and trips for which 'voluntary contributions' are required
- inadequate nutritional levels
- ill health, affecting school attendance
- overcrowding, making home study difficult
- insufficient money for books and aids such as computers, music lessons and private tuition
- greater family stress and breakdown, with fewer resources to cope
- cost of transport to school (meaning that the closest school might have to be chosen)
- cost of continuing education after the age of 16

In addition, those living in local education authorities in poorer areas might be disadvantaged by:
- little free pre-school provision
- poorly funded schools, because of multiple problems locally
- schools being less able to buy resources through parental contributions and fund-raising

Smith and Noble argue that two types of reform are needed to extend educational opportunities to children of all social backgrounds:
- Poverty needs to be alleviated by measures such as increasing the minimum wage and child benefits. This would be more helpful than the present uneven and sometimes stigmatising provision of free school meals and grants for uniforms.

- A more concerted effort needs to be made to improve education in poor districts. This has been attempted through compensatory education schemes. An example is the creation of education priority areas in the late 1960s when, in a drive to improve literacy, the government gave extra money to four urban areas so they could expand pre-school education, attract more teachers and equip schools better. Results were disappointing. Insufficient funds were made available and parents' support was not enlisted — they should have been advised on how to help their children.

Since 1998, the government has funded education action zones to raise standards in clusters of schools in disadvantaged areas, through initiatives such as breakfast and after-school clubs (Chapter 6). Smith and Noble, however, suggest a more comprehensive programme for poorer areas, including:
- high-quality, affordable pre-school provision
- special reading schemes
- reduction in class sizes for young children
- more effective schools, with greater parental involvement

They argue that since the 1980s, government attention has shifted from equality of educational opportunity to parental choice and financial encouragement to schools to raise standards. Middle-class parents are better able to recognise and select the best schools for their children, with the result that working-class children have to make do with less successful, poorly funded schools.

Are attainment differences due to class cultures?

Some sociologists have claimed that cultural deprivation, different attitudes to education, less satisfactory ways of bringing up children and language deficiencies result in poorer attainment for many working-class children. These views are extremely controversial and it is difficult to separate such factors entirely from the effects of low income.

Child-rearing practices

Beginning in 1946, J. W. B. Douglas carried out a longitudinal survey of over 5000 children from birth to the age of 11, which is described in *The Home and the School*. He then tracked most of the children to the age of 16, for a second publication, *All Our Future*. The surveys indicated that middle-class parents were more likely to stimulate young children in ways that helped their learning, rewarding them for improving skills in a wide range of areas from speech to games, so that they became achievement orientated. They were more likely to encourage older children to aim high and stay at school beyond the minimum age. Such parents seemed to show more interest in their children's school, as they were more likely to attend parents' evenings.

However, the working-class parents might have been unable to afford for their children to stay on at school. Perhaps they did not attend parents' evenings because they worked night shifts or felt uncomfortable visiting a school. There are many variables to consider. Though the study is dated, the focus on parental encouragement is interesting.

Chris Gaine and Rosalyn George, in *Gender, 'Race' and Class in Schooling* (1999), identify practical reasons why children of working-class parents may under-achieve:

> If parents were not successful at school themselves, if they are not confident with the written word...then they are unlikely to be confident in this kind of activity. When their children have homework involving comprehension, research or working in a foreign language they may feel a gap between wanting to help and knowing the best way to do so. This is not to say that computers, homework clubs, relatives and advice cannot get round these obstacles, but they are obstacles nevertheless, and ones not experienced by parents who are, say, accountants or managers. These obstacles are increased if the parents have low levels of literacy themselves.
>
> C. Gaine and R. George, *Gender, 'Race' and Class in Schooling* (1999)

Cultural capital

Marxist Pierre Bourdieu suggests that middle-class children have more cultural capital. He collected information from surveys conducted in France in the late 1960s and the 1970s to analyse how often members of different occupational groups visited theatres, concerts and museums and listened to classical music. He also recorded the types of newspapers, books and films they liked.

Many of these activities require a good income and there was a strong correlation between higher class and regular consumption of high or 'dominant' culture. This 'linguistic and cultural competence' was passed on to the children, who did better in the education system because 'the culture which it transmits is closer to the dominant culture'.

Those at the top of the social ladder can afford to buy this sort of culture and pass it to their children. This is known as cultural reproduction. The result is that the children succeed at school and eventually obtain employment as good as that of their parents — social reproduction.

Task 2.2

How relevant are Bourdieu's ideas to modern Britain?

Guidance

Consider the following:

- Examination specifications are based more on the high culture familiar to many middle-class children, such as the works of Shakespeare and classical composers, than they are on the popular and mass culture associated with the working class.
- Nowadays, most museums and art galleries have free entry and socially diverse audiences can access Shakespeare and serious literature through television adaptations. Many middle-class people prefer 'soap operas' to opera. The mass media are said to have reduced the cultural gap between the classes.

Michael Young in *Knowledge and Control* (1971) agrees that those in power — the dominant classes — regard their own type of knowledge as important and include it in examination specifications. Those with cultural capital — people with similar background and knowledge — are more likely to succeed in the system. Theoretically, any subject could be equally worthy of study. However, in practice, classical and European languages are more likely to be taught in British schools than Asian languages, abstract subjects are more heavily timetabled than practical ones, assessment depends more on literacy than on oral skills and social sciences are often excluded altogether, perhaps because of their potentially subversive nature.

Speech patterns

In the 1960s, Basil Bernstein began work on the way speech patterns appear to vary with class. He distinguished two types of speech:

- **Restricted code** involves limited vocabulary, incomplete and disjointed sentence structure and lack of explanation. It relies on the listener already knowing what is being spoken about.
- **Elaborated code** has varied vocabulary and is grammatically structured. Sufficient details and explanations are given for anyone listening to understand.

According to Bernstein, middle-class pupils may speak restricted code to intimates, but they use elaborated code at school where it is rewarded by teachers who use it themselves. It is closer to the language of textbooks and essays than restricted code, which is all that working-class children use with ease.

Inevitably, Bernstein's work has met with opposition. Besides the dangers of generalising about whole classes (which applies throughout this topic), problems arise when middle-class researchers record working-class speech. In a parallel situation, William Labov showed that black children spoke in a restricted way when formally interviewed by a white researcher, but talked far more fluently when sitting on the floor with a black researcher and a bag of crisps.

In 1984, Barbara Tizard and colleagues tape-recorded pre-school working-class and middle-class girls talking at home and at nursery school to test the 'deficit model' of the verbally deprived child. They found that the working-class girls displayed extensive and sometimes sophisticated skills when speaking to their mothers but used restricted language with staff at nursery. They suggested this was because working-class children tended to receive less contact, stimulation and encouragement from the staff. This relates to the concept of teacher labelling that will be discussed in Chapter 5.

In line with Bernstein, Denis Lawton (*Social Class, Language and Education*, 1968) agreed that a great deal of working-class potential is being wasted, partly as a result of 'inadequacy of linguistic range and control'. He conducted written language tests, group discussions and individual interviews with boys of secondary-school age and found class differences similar to Bernstein's, with the gap increasing between the ages of 12 and 15. Lawton disagreed with critics who regarded attempts to change working-class children's 'authentic' speech as a form of 'interference'; he believed that education must aim to extend children's experiences.

> There is the simple socioeconomic fact that traditional working-class socialisation processes are preparing its members for a world which is disappearing. In the near future, routine manual jobs are going to disappear and jobs which will become available in industry or in the bureaucratic, welfare or distribution spheres will require a much higher level of symbolic control (verbal skills).

Cultural deprivation and class attitudes

Linking with the ideas above is the notion of cultural deprivation. This suggests that those at the bottom of the class structure lack the values and attitudes needed for educational success. Stimulating books and toys are absent not merely because people cannot afford them but because they do not realise their importance. According to the American anthropologist Oscar Lewis, the most disadvantaged people are sunk in a 'culture of poverty', which makes them unable to take advantage of opportunities that arise. Barry Sugarman (1970) identified similar values among the British working class. His findings are summarised in Table 2.1.

Table 2.1 Social class values according to Sugarman

Working class	Middle class
Immediate gratification — leaving school as soon as possible for the rewards of pay and freedom from discipline	**Deferred gratification** — postponing wages and leisure, realising that effort given to study will bring greater rewards later
Present time orientation — the unpredictable life of the poor means long-term planning is inappropriate	**Planning** — the acquisition of qualifications and skills appropriate to a career
Fatalism — resigning themselves to a lowly fate instead of trying to improve it; social closure (the inaccessibility of higher positions) is accepted	**Taking control** — of own learning; overcoming obstacles with determination and confidence; society viewed as a **meritocracy** with ambition reaping rewards
Collectivism — poorer people have been most influential when united in a group, such as a trade union; school subcultures distract from personal success	**Individualism** — school requires individual effort and competition between students
Them and us — people of higher status are viewed as snobs or not macho enough; this discourages upward mobility	**Climbing the social ladder** — encouraged

Task 2.3

How relevant are Sugarman's ideas to modern Britain?

Guidance

Consider the following:

- Fewer people now live in communities that are centred around a particular kind of work, such as mining. There is greater geographical and social mobility.
- Postmodernists argue that we have multiple sources of identity — for example, gender, sexuality, ethnicity and age group. Social class is only one influence.
- Ray Gosling describes British social structure as 'middle-class porridge'. Very few people now view themselves as working class and most aspire to middle-class consumption patterns. The adoption of middle-class behaviour patterns by people of a working-class background is known as **embourgeoisement**.
- Access courses, primarily designed to encourage working-class people without qualifications to apply to higher education, are far more often taken up by middle-class students. Is this evidence of working-class fatalism?

Positional theory

French sociologist Raymond Boudon in *Education, Opportunity and Social Inequality* (1974) makes a similar point about class attitudes to that of Sugarman. Working-class pupils may not wish to become members of the middle class. If they are academically ambitious, they will suffer from social isolation, perhaps being the only member of their peer group to stay on at school or go to university. Relationships with their relatives may become stilted as education changes their lifestyle and tastes. In contrast, middle-class pupils are motivated to work hard in order to remain in the same group as their friends; to be downwardly mobile would be humiliating. Parental attitudes reinforce these tendencies. Professional parents pressurise their young to maintain a similar social position, whereas working-class parents frequently accept that their children will take working-class jobs.

The interviews conducted by Gillian Plummer in *Failing Working-Class Girls* (2000) support Boudon's observations. She recorded the experiences of girls from manual backgrounds who were among the minority accepted by grammar schools or who were successful enough in non-selective schools to continue their education through A-levels and teacher training college or university.

> Academic success brought home/school disharmony and conflict. For instance, the needs and aspirations developed in school distanced many successful working-class girls from their family: 'It increasingly set me apart…even from my mother, who had been a major instrument in winning this new life for me'. At the same time, family needs were a constant threat. The pressure to conform, 'to leave school and go into the mill or factory, to get a chap, was unremitting'.
>
> G. Plummer, *Failing Working-Class Girls* (2000)

These conflicts explain why so few pupils continued school beyond the minimum leaving age. Family poverty meant that they stood out in their home-made uniforms, were reprimanded when they failed to bring expensive cookery ingredients, could not go on school trips, have music lessons or take school friends home. They had to take paid work in the evenings and holidays. Their accents and grammar were noticed by staff and pupils, which caused isolation and loss of self-esteem.

> At school I felt ashamed of my background and attempted to conceal it. My dad was a manual worker and we were pretty poor and I didn't want my classmates to know this. Nor did I want them to know I lived in a 'rough' area, in a house that didn't have a bathroom.
>
> Quoted in G. Plummer, *Failing Working-Class Girls* (2000)

The school curriculum reflected middle-class lifestyles in its reading schemes and the type of subject matter expected in written tasks.

I had always hated writing the stories that were required…about trips out or holidays. I hadn't been on holiday and outings were rare and unmemorable events. The significant events in my life were traumatic family illnesses, a father temporarily out of work, the burden of too many domestic responsibilities. Other activities like playing on the railway embankment, trespassing on derelict land, street fights, scrumping, all of them acts of deviance, could not be talked about in school…Somehow I knew that these were not the topics being sought under the heading, 'Write about what you did at the weekend'.

G. Plummer, *Failing Working-Class Girls* (2000)

Plummer's respondents found that 'learning for working-class students is simultaneously about learning to be middle class'. However, that made it increasingly difficult to fit in with their home community, relatives and old friends. Being seen in school uniform on the journey home was sufficient to draw verbal abuse and harassment from working-class boys, who resented their rejection of the traditional female role. If their parents were unaware of the benefits of continuing education or saw it as the duty of children to contribute to the family finances, there was little chance of bright girls fulfilling their potential.

There was always the pull of wanting to do what other working-class girls of my age were doing — acting the grown up. I was in pubs at 15, at late-night dances at 16, in nightclubs at 17. The pull of this more exciting life, which mitigated our isolation from local working-class peers, created huge conflict for those of us who stayed on at school. Working-class students have still to be assimilated into a culture where it is normal to stay on at school until 18.

G. Plummer, *Failing Working-Class Girls* (2000)

Task 2.4

Can class attitudes and income factors be separated?

Guidance

Consider the following:

- The problems that Plummer's working-class respondents had with fitting into selective education and staying at school beyond the minimum leaving age.
- The 'impostor syndrome' experienced by working-class girls at university. 'Higher education institutions are still geared to middle-class and upper-class students' needs and are relatively unwelcoming to working-class students and the knowledge they bring' (Plummer).
- Educational maintenance awards have been available since 2004 for students from low-income families who are doing post-16 academic and vocational courses at school and colleges of further education.
- The recent imposition of university tuition fees. Though loans are available, working-class students are discouraged by the thought of years of debt. Middle-class parents can often afford to help their children meet university expenses.

Do independent schools increase the attainment gap?

According to subcultural studies carried out by Paul Willis, Stephen Ball, John Abraham and others in state-run education, anti-school attitudes are more likely to develop among working-class students. In addition, streaming may to some extent reflect social class and result in poorer behaviour and motivation by students placed in lower streams. Teachers may consequently expect poorer results from such groups, even labelling them as unlikely to succeed. These issues are discussed fully in Chapter 5.

Despite the remaining social class attainment gap, state education has developed over the centuries to cater increasingly for the needs of working-class children. In contrast, the independent school system remains largely the preserve of the affluent.

A glance at the origins of the most successful people in Britain reveals that few of them attended comprehensives — most were educated in independent schools. These are fee-paying schools not controlled by the government. They include famous old public schools such as Eton, Rugby and Harrow. These were established to train young men to take up important positions in society. It is said that the Battle of Waterloo was won on the playing fields of Eton. In other words, students were taught qualities — such as self-discipline, physical toughness and willingness to make personal sacrifices to benefit the group — that helped them to defend their country.

Eton schoolboys, including Prince Harry

Nowadays, a higher proportion of pupils from independent schools than from state schools obtain good A-levels and enter Oxford and Cambridge universities. An 'Oxbridge' education can open doors to top jobs in the civil service, law, the armed forces and similar professions. Even without top qualifications, students from public schools may obtain good jobs through the 'old-boy network'. At interview, they may be identified by their 'old school ties' and favoured by employers from the same or a similar school.

Most of the students attending independent schools are middle or upper class. The fees are too high for working-class parents to afford, unless their children win scholarships. It is traditional for the privileged to send their children to independent schools, to be educated as gentlemen or ladies. Reasons for public schools' academic success include smaller class sizes, better facilities, longer hours and more orderly behaviour — parents may withdraw their children if the atmosphere is unsatisfactory.

Some independent schools are founded for specific purposes — for example, to promote particular skills, religions or philosophies. Choir schools, faith schools, progressive schools such as Summerhill and charitable foundations set up to educate the children of particular occupations (e.g. merchant seamen) are less likely to draw most of their students from upper-class backgrounds.

In an attempt to address criticism that the independent school system is socially divisive, the Conservative Party introduced the Assisted Places Scheme in 1980, to pay towards the fees of poorer but able children. Labour discontinued the 'elitist' scheme in 1997, setting up education action zones for the disadvantaged instead.

Should independent schools be abolished?

Opponents of the independent system argue as follows:
- It creams off some of the more able from state schools, which means that a truly comprehensive system is not achievable. Only 7–8% of all students attend independent schools.
- If their own children enjoy independent education, the ruling classes lack the motivation to improve state schools.
- The system perpetuates divisions in society. Students at public school have the unfair advantage of sponsored mobility.
- There is less state control over what is taught because following the national curriculum is not compulsory.

Defenders of the independent system say the following:
- Parents sending children to independent schools still pay (through taxes) for the state education system that they do not use. Funding for state schools would be more thinly spread if independent schools were abolished.
- If people wish to spend their own money on education, they should be free to do so.
- Independent schools are part of British tradition. Successful schools should be left alone.

- Some independent schools are needed to offer choice and variety, for religious minorities and parents who prefer progressive, alternative or boarding education.

Those who dislike the national curriculum, or other aspects of government education policy, would probably find the last of the above points the most convincing.

There is evidence that some of the less prestigious independent schools are becoming more like state schools as they experience competition and financial problems. They are taking more day-pupils than boarders, becoming co-educational, offering special-needs facilities and are less keen to expel students for bad behaviour. Their resources, both in terms of staff and equipment, are often stretched. The opportunities offered by less well-known independent schools may compare poorly with those at successful state schools.

Research suggestions

- Interview students from independent and state schools to see how their experience of school differ. Also, compare their class backgrounds by asking about their parents' occupations.
- Interview Year 11 comprehensive school students about whether they intend to stay on for A-levels and the reasons for their choice. Are their decisions most closely linked with the length of their parents' education, the family's ability to fund continued education or their progress in school and personal ambitions?

Ethics and optimum conditions for conducting interviews need to be considered when phrasing these sensitive questions.

Which factors are most responsible for working-class underachievement?

There is widespread agreement among sociologists about the amount of working-class potential that is unfulfilled in the education system. However, opinions differ about the reasons why this occurs. One issue is the wide variation in the quality of schools, meaning that prosperous students have the choice of independent, selective or top-class comprehensive schools while those living in poor districts tend to go to the closest — sometimes 'failing' — school. Whether the locality offers effective compensatory education, free nurseries and schemes such as Excellence in Cities for gifted children is a related aspect of government policy. Smith and Noble have expressed strong views about the need for better pre-school provision and smaller classes in poorer areas.

Another issue is what happens within schools. Setting, the formation of subcultures and the effect of teacher expectations are covered in Chapter 5. Plummer and Young noted middle-class bias in the school curriculum and this links closely with Bourdieu's notion of cultural capital.

Bernstein and Lawton suggest that restricted language skills hold back working-class children, but Plummer strongly disagrees with the idea that their language is inferior.

> The all-pervasive social pathology model — inadequate working class homes, language and culture — is still with us. It continues to distract attention from the ideological purpose of perceiving working-class values, behaviour etc. as 'deficient' instead of different and from a serious analysis of the structural conditions which promote differences, exploitation and oppression. Even those who conform and master institutionalised knowledge go on to face inequalities in higher education and the job market.
>
> G. Plummer, *Failing Working-Class Girls* (2000)

In Plummer's opinion, low income is the main cause of educational disadvantage. It often correlates with parental unemployment, poor mental and physical health and overcrowding, so that children are expected to help at home or to take paid work instead of concentrating on homework and staying on at school. The fatalistic attitudes noted by Sugarman might well accompany these structural inequalities because these are survival mechanisms of an oppressed working class. Like Smith and Noble, Plummer believes that, while economic inequalities remain, the educational achievements of working-class children are unlikely to match those of the higher classes. Thus, bright, working-class children take insecure poorly paid jobs and their children inherit the same problems, so the cycle of poverty continues.

Summary

- There are major differences in educational achievements between social classes, with far fewer working-class children going to university. Educational success affects adult lifestyles greatly.
- Low income influences progress at school and the chances of staying at school beyond the minimum age.
- Differences in child-rearing practices between social classes and parents' own level of education and cultural capital are likely to affect children's attainment.

- Sociologists disagree about the significance of class differences in linguistic skills and whether or not the working class are 'culturally deprived'.
- Changes in the class structure may make differences in class attitudes to education less polarised than in the past. However, Plummer's recent study suggests that academically successful working-class children still risk social stigmatisation from their peers.
- There is pressure on children of the middle and working classes to remain at the same social level as their parents.
- Factors within schools, including the middle-class nature of the curriculum, may further explain differential attainment.
- The availability of different quality schooling to different classes is a significant factor. Independent schools are accessible mainly to affluent families and tend to produce better academic results than state schools.
- Many sociologists reject cultural explanations for working-class under-achievement as 'victim-blaming' and argue that the gap cannot be closed without major structural changes to alleviate poverty.

Task 2.5

Answer the following short questions:

(a) Explain what is meant by cultural capital. (2 marks)

(b) Suggest *two* reasons, apart from lack of interest, why many working-class parents may fail to attend parents' evenings. (4 marks)

Guidance

(a) Avoid using a similar word, such as 'culture', in your explanation. A clear definition is needed. A brief example may make your meaning clearer.

(b) ● No more than *two* well-expressed and thoughtful sentences are needed for each reason.

● Ensure that your reasons are quite different from each other.

● The section 'Child-rearing practices' should be helpful.

Useful websites

- Sociology Stuff — click on 'Education', then select 'Inequality class' from a box entitled 'Course notes'
  www.homestead.com/rouncefield/frontpage.html
- Child Poverty Action Group
  www.cpag.org.uk/campaigns/AtGreatestRisk/AtGreatestRisk_conclusion.pdf

- Social Class and Higher Education: issues affecting decisions on participation by lower social class groups
  www.employment-studies.co.uk/summary/summary.php?id=rr267
- SociologyOnline UK — click on 'Poverty'
  www.sociologyonline.co.uk/soc_essays/Poverty.htm

Further reading

- Gaine, C. and George, R. (1999) *Gender, 'Race' and Class in Schooling: A New Introduction*, Falmer Press.
- Plummer, G. (2000) *Failing Working-class Girls*, Trentham Books.
- Smith, T. and Noble, M. (1995) *Education Divides: Poverty and Schooling in the 1990s*, Child Poverty Action Group.

Does gender influence educational attainment?

What are the patterns of male and female attainment?

A few years ago, girls outperformed boys in primary-school tests and in examinations at 16, but fewer girls than boys stayed on at school for A-levels. Those who did, tended to take fewer subjects, so they were less eligible for university. The situation has now changed, with girls overtaking boys in the later years of education as well as in early key stage tests, particularly in English.

Examine the differences in attainment levels shown in Figures 3.1 and 3.2.

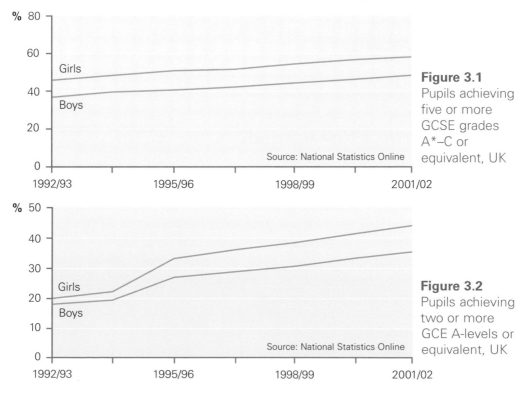

Figure 3.1 Pupils achieving five or more GCSE grades A*–C or equivalent, UK

Source: National Statistics Online

Figure 3.2 Pupils achieving two or more GCE A-levels or equivalent, UK

Source: National Statistics Online

In the UK, girls generally outperform boys at GCSE and A-level. In 2001–02:
- 58% of girls in their last year of compulsory education achieved five or more GCSE grades A*–C, compared with 47% of boys
- 43% of girls gained two or more A-levels (or equivalent), compared with 34% of boys

Over recent years, the proportion of students of both sexes gaining two or more GCE A-levels (or equivalent) has increased, so it would be untrue to suggest that boys are performing worse than they did in the past. However, between 1992/93 and 2001/02, the proportion of girls gaining this result more than doubled — from 20% to 43%. The equivalent boys' increase was from 18% to 34%.

At A-level, girls outperformed boys in virtually all subject groups in 2000/01 and almost twice as many girls as boys obtained distinctions in Advanced GNVQs.

At first degree level in 2002, results were:
- first class — 10% of males, 9% of females
- upper-second class — 40% of males, 49% of females

Females now make up almost 60% of students in full-time higher education.

Why did girls underachieve in the past?

Until recently, feminist sociologists were anxious to investigate why girls dropped out of the educational system.

Reasons suggested for underachievement

Differential access

School curricula used to be divided along gender lines, with girls directed into home economics and other 'feminine' subjects, in preparation for domestic roles. Women were not admitted to any British university until 1877; Cambridge did not fully recognise women students until 1947. Before the national curriculum was introduced in 1988, girls often opted out of sciences and languages early, in favour of less academically prestigious subjects such as child development and European studies.

Patriarchal ideology

To retain male power in society, women were directed into domesticity. Many Victorians believed that for women to compete with men was unnatural and this attitude persisted until the raising of feminist consciousness in the 1970s. J. W. B. Douglas, researching in the 1960s, found that families still gave financial priority to their sons' education.

Socialisation of girls

In 1974, the feminist Ann Oakley examined the social construction of gender roles in Western societies and concluded that feminine behaviour is not innate but is a result of primary socialisation. Until recently, parents unthinkingly gave girls miniature domestic items, dolls and soft toys to play with. This 'canalised' them into accepting domestic and caring roles. Boys received construction kits and chemistry sets, which gave them practice in spatial and scientific reasoning and, therefore, better preparation for schoolwork. Oakley also noted the 'manipulation' of children's self-concepts through the way that parents dressed their children and paid more attention to girls' appearance. Children were made continually aware of gender differences through appellations such as 'good girl' and 'brave boy'. They modelled themselves on same-sex adults, a trend reinforced by media stereotyping and sexist practices at nursery and school.

A girl with her new doll

Task 3.1

Except in households where parents ban certain types of toys, little girls are still more inclined to play indoors with soft toys and dolls, nursing them or making tea for them and playing shops and schools, while boys run round outside 'shooting' each other and digging holes in the ground. However, many young women now reject early domestic roles in favour of academic success and a career. How might their early play prepare them for schoolwork better than boys?

Guidance

Boys are said to have a shorter attention span than girls. They find it difficult to sit still in the classroom. Girls are more advanced at language skills and find it easier to express their ideas on paper. Consider how the games described above relate to these attributes.

The research by Murphy and Elwood (Table 3.1, page 48) will provide further ideas.

The ideology of romance

In separate studies in the 1970s, Sue Sharpe and Angela McRobbie found that working-class teenage girls were unambitious at school because their sights were set on early marriage and childbearing. They only expected to work for a short time, so they had no incentive to obtain good qualifications. Girls in their early teens were preoccupied with pop idols and dance steps, preparing themselves for courtship. In later teens, they often formed anti-school subcultures, doing their hair and comparing dates in lessons.

In 1994, Sue Sharpe again interviewed girls from a similar background. She found quite different attitudes, which are described in *Just like a Girl*. The girls were more interested in education and a career and less confident that marriage and childbearing would bring them happiness.

Invisible girls in the classroom

Michelle Stanworth, Dale Spender and Jane French all found girls to be disadvantaged in classroom interactions. Teachers spent less time with girls, knew fewer names, allowed boys to insult girls and predicted less ambitious careers, even for very able girls. Boys dominated oral work. Alison Kelly noted how boys rushed for the limited apparatus available in science lessons, meaning that girls could sometimes only watch as experiments were performed.

Differences in confidence

Attitudes of pupils were also significant. In *Gender and Schooling* (1983), Stanworth reports that sixth formers of both sexes, when asked to estimate the test scores of others, underestimated those of girls and overestimated those of boys.

Licht and Dweck (1987), noted that boys were reprimanded more for bad behaviour; consequently, boys attributed poor results to lack of effort. This had little effect on their self-esteem. In contrast, girls receiving low marks blamed their own lack of ability, which sapped their confidence. When faced with a new learning task, they had lower expectations of success and so tended to avoid challenges.

Hidden curriculum

Until recently, reading books and textbooks tended to show boys and girls in stereotypical roles, as Glenys Lobban found in her study of six reading schemes in 1974. In the stories she examined, girls were occupied with skipping, preparing tea and caring for younger siblings; boys rescued people, explored and built things. Adult females were only shown in the roles of relatives, teachers or shop assistants, whereas males were represented in 15 different roles. Though there has since been a conscious effort by some authors to write stories reversing traditional gender roles, a study by Lesley Best in 1992 of 132 pre-school readers found the position not much changed, with 71% heroes compared with 26% heroines.

In 1985, Alison Kelly noted that females were seldom included in science textbooks; when they did appear, it was in sex-stereotyped roles emphasising their marginalised position in science. Though sociologists disagree about the extent to which people are influenced by representations in the media and similar sources, there are concerns that young children in particular are likely to have their ideas shaped by such messages.

Blue Lantern Studio/Corbis

In the story of Rapunzel, the male is the rescuer

Why have girls' achievements improved?

There is evidence that girls in single-sex schools outperform those in mixed schools, perhaps indicating that the male domination and teacher bias outlined in the above studies still operate. However, as girls now excel at every level except for the acquisition of higher degrees (Masters degrees and PhDs), sociologists are more interested in what has happened in recent years to boost their progress. Suggestions include the following:

- Equal rights legislation and feminism have encouraged the mothers of the present generation of teenagers to work for a greater part of their lives. They act as role models, showing that qualifications and training are worthwhile.
- Increased marriage breakdown has demonstrated the need for female economic independence.
- Many parents and most teachers now believe that girls as well as boys should achieve all they can. This has made girls more ambitious. Many no longer give priority to marriage and domesticity.
- The 11-plus examination required a higher pass mark for girls, because boys were assumed to be late developers. Many able girls were sent to secondary modern schools. When the comprehensive system became widespread, able girls were able to work at levels matching their potential.
- In 1988, coursework became a significant part of many GCSEs. Girls tend to put more effort into coursework than boys.
- Equal opportunity initiatives have encouraged girls to fulfil their potential in traditionally masculine subjects. Schemes include Girls into Science and

Technology, Take your Daughter to Work, Women into Science and Engineering, Girls in Aerospace, and Computer Clubs for Girls. Schools are trying harder to eradicate sexist assumptions and teaching materials and may display posters about female achievers. Some girls' schools have become specialist schools for science, mathematics, technology and engineering.

- The national curriculum ensures that girls cannot drop science and technology before the age of 16. Until 1988, it was not compulsory for students to study three sciences to the end of key stage 4.
- Traditional male jobs in heavy manual work are disappearing, whereas new 'female' opportunities in service industries and information technology are being created. These require teamwork and communication skills that are more often associated with women.
- The media have latched onto evidence of female success. Television programmes about ambitious girls and failing boys may influence the self-images of the sexes.

Closing the gender gap

Madeleine Arnot (1999) elaborates on the reasons why many girls have improved their performance recently. Increasing geographical mobility and the loosening of inter-generational family ties have encouraged people to forge their own destinies. Middle-class girls entered universities in increasing numbers from the 1960s. This resulted in more women teachers in secondary schools, many of whom disseminated feminist ideals and encouraged girls of all classes to be ambitious. They gradually dispelled the 'fear of success' that caused many girls to underachieve, afraid that being too clever would make them unattractive to men. The Sex Discrimination Act (1975), the contraceptive pill and labour-saving devices in the home made well-paid extended careers more feasible. The new entrepreneurial culture, with icons such as Anita Roddick, Martha Lane Fox and Michelle Mone, has encouraged more girls to study economics and commercial subjects in order to enter the business world.

Anita Roddick, founder of The Body Shop

Several studies of Afro-Caribbean girls have found them ambitious to gain qualifications in order to avoid either dependence on men or having to resort to the unskilled jobs often associated with their ethnic group. In 1996, T. N. Basit found Asian Muslim girls who were being supported in their ambitions to be lawyers, doctors, accountants and pharmacists, even though many of their fathers were either unemployed or manual workers. Many working-class white girls want to be 'new traditional' women, enjoying a stable family life and having interesting employment at the same time.

Despite these signs of success, Arnot makes the following points:

- As many girls as boys leave school without qualifications or the prospect of work.
- Working-class girls still choose stereotypically feminine training courses. They may opt for poorly paid work in caring and domestic fields in order to avoid stressful work contexts and harassment by men.
- Female university students tend to avoid science, technology, IT and mathematics. The careers associated with their preferred options of arts, social sciences and education often lead to less prestigious feminised professions.

To summarise: the qualifications girls gain do not necessarily create a shift away from conventional class and gender roles.

Why are some boys underachieving?

Mitsos and Browne (1998) have suggested various reasons for boys' lower academic achievements.

- Boys are more easily distracted in the classroom. It is not regarded as macho to work hard, so they 'play up' to impress friends. Hard-working boys may be accused of effeminacy or homosexuality.
- Teachers tolerate a lower standard of work and worse classroom behaviour from males, expecting that 'boys will be boys'. As their behaviour becomes intolerable, they are likely to be sent out of lessons. Boys are four times more likely than girls to be permanently excluded from school.
- Boys spend less time on homework. Parents can encourage this difference by playing outdoor games with boys and reading with girls. Older girls are more likely to engage in hobbies that complement their schoolwork, especially language-based activities.
- Recent psychological research by Dennis Molfese suggests that girls are born with greater ability to distinguish sounds, which puts them ahead in reading and writing.

- Parents think it is unnatural for little boys to be 'swots' and wrongly assume the gender gap will close later.
- There has been a decline in male manual work as Britain has switched from predominantly manufacturing industries to service industries. In the past, boys were sometimes motivated to try hard at school because they needed jobs to support their wives. If women now take the better jobs and prefer single parenthood to having to support unemployed husbands, young men are less motivated to work for qualifications or to resist involvement in crime. According to this theory, there has been a reversal in the self-esteem of the sexes, with boys now prone to failure. However, Mairtin Mac an Ghaill's research, discussed below, suggests this is an oversimplification.
- Many boys overestimate their own abilities leading up to GCSE and do not work hard enough because they expect good results. This theory is at odds with the male loss of self-esteem described previously.
- Boys have difficulty organising their time to meet deadlines. This may be because girls have the role model of mothers who have to organise the home, fitting in domestic responsibilities and paid work. Most fathers' lives involve less multi-tasking.

Gendered learning outside and inside school

Following on from Ann Oakley's work on canalisation, in the 1990s Patricia Murphy and Jannette Elwood collected data from their own and other studies to see how the early activities of each sex translated into skills and aptitudes for particular school subjects. Their findings are summarised in Table 3.1.

Table 3.1 Gendered learning

Finding	Implication
Boys in nursery showed an early interest in machinery. Staff steered them towards reading books about vehicles.	Boys become more familiar with factual books than stories, so they are less likely to enjoy fictional reading schemes. They then struggle to produce their own imaginative, extended writing as required in English and humanities. They therefore become alienated from important primary school activities.
At nursery, girls were more interested in drawing.	Girls learn pencil control sooner, getting ahead with writing.

Finding	Implication
When given Lego bricks, infant boys were more inclined to build things with wheels and movable parts. Girls built houses that they used for role play.	Boys gain greater confidence in practical aspects of science and technology, whereas girls enjoy communication, which is relevant to most subjects.
By the end of primary school, girls were less keen on mathematics than when they started school and boys were less keen on reading and writing.	Girls' lack of confidence in mathematics leads to their being disproportionately entered for middle tiers, meaning that they cannot earn the B grade often required to continue to A-level. In English GCSE coursework, teachers reward narrative and descriptive writing over the more factual genres that boys tend to produce.
By the end of primary school, boys were less concerned about being reprimanded, while girls were anxious to obey and please their teachers.	By the mid-teens, peer pressure on boys not to work hard may impact on their performance at GCSE.

Are schools still male-dominated?

The male-dominated vocational curriculum

In *The Making of Men: Masculinities, Sexualities and Schooling* (1994) Mac an Ghaill argues that, in often subtle ways, many schools are dominated by heterosexual masculinity. The needs of girls and homosexual students are marginalised, despite school strategies to address sex-role socialisation through changing texts and offering less traditional careers advice.

He suggests that, since the educational reforms in the 1980s that encouraged emphasis on technology and ICT and competition between schools for funding, schools may have become more 'masculine' (see Chapter 6). In his 3-year ethnographic study of Parnell School, a co-educational Midlands comprehensive, he identified about 40% of teachers as 'new entrepreneurs'. This powerful, predominantly male group consisted of department heads of vocationally orientated subjects such as business and computer studies. They saw the school's role as training students in new technology and competition in business, were personally ambitious and wanted to market the school and attract commercial sponsorship.

Other teachers, such as the 'old collectivists' — committed to pastoral care, liberal values, anti-sexism and anti-racism — were eclipsed by this group, as the timetable and funding were reorganised to promote ICT, business studies and technology in line with the government promotion of 'new vocationalism'. Teachers running these high-status subjects viewed interested boys of reasonable potential as their ideal students. These 'new-enterprise boys' were mainly the children of skilled manual workers — boys who in the past would have learnt manual trades through apprenticeship schemes. They realised that the best opportunities for them now were in ICT roles in the service industries, gaining appropriate skills through school projects and carefully chosen work experience placements. They were shaped by 'the modern mode of masculinity that was in the ascendancy within the school', i.e. a competitive business ethic. Mac an Ghaill quotes Davies (1992) in describing how males dominate promising areas.

> In terms of hierarchy of knowledge, males have exerted control by designating certain knowledge areas as simultaneously high status and masculine (currently science, maths, technology, but not so long ago, modern languages). It is interesting how particularly promising knowledge areas get 'captured' by the 'dominant', and reworked to show tendencies in their favour. Hence keyboard skills were once dismissed as typing or at best office skills, and designated female; now with computerisation, they are called intermediate technology, and as we all know, are better done by males.
>
> Davies, quoted in M. Mac an Ghaill *The Making of Men: Masculinities, Sexualities and Schooling* (1994)

Mac an Ghaill's findings contrast with previous studies that suggested that middle-class girls and boys are teachers' preferred students. At Parnell, girls of all social classes were marginalised by the enterprise culture, as were women teachers. Though a computer club had been organised to interest girls in ICT, it soon became dominated by new enterprise boys, so the girls deserted it. When girls and female teachers complained about the domination of these vocational courses by boys, male teachers justified it because male employment prospects in the area were poorer. They made 'essentialist' comments that boys have 'more interest in machines and technical matters'.

In contrast, many working-class girls were steered into care-orientated vocational courses. Some complained that this was pointless because they already had experience of caring for siblings and sick relatives at home.

> *Kerry*: When he (teacher) asked me what I had learnt, I told him, 'I've learnt that you are trying to make us housewives'. He went mad, saying that we were learning lots of new skills. That's rubbish, it's just common sense; to us anyway. They should be teaching us things that will help us to get a real job.
>
> Quoted in M. Mac an Ghaill *The Making of Men: Masculinities, Sexualities and Schooling* (1994)

These experiences of the school's gendered hidden curriculum suggest that media claims that the 'future is female' are exaggerated.

Boys tend to monopolise computers

TopFoto

Task 3.2

In the account of a study on students that follows, Mac an Ghaill identifies five groups and also describes the experiences of homosexuals. Make a chart with a column for each group's attributes and experiences to help you focus on his analysis, in which group names are in bold.

Differentiated masculinities and femininities

As well as challenging the view that education now favours girls, Mac an Ghaill's study revealed various male subcultures with different attitudes to schoolwork. In addition to the ambitious **new-enterprise students**, who could be likened to Paul Willis's 'ear'oles', he identified a downwardly mobile working-class group, similar in attitudes to Willis's 'lads'. These **macho lads** were in the bottom two sets for all subjects, either because they had been placed there from the start or because they had been demoted. They viewed the school as 'a system of hostile authority and meaningless work demands'. Their academic failure, poor prospects of finding manual work locally and close surveillance by teachers who viewed them as troublemakers, led them into aggressive behaviour to preserve their self-esteem.

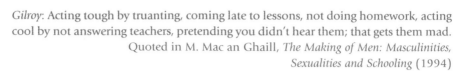

Gilroy: Acting tough by truanting, coming late to lessons, not doing homework, acting cool by not answering teachers, pretending you didn't hear them; that gets them mad.

Quoted in M. Mac an Ghaill, *The Making of Men: Masculinities, Sexualities and Schooling* (1994)

The macho lads associated the studies they failed in with inferior effeminacy, rejected schoolwork as inappropriate for them as men and bullied other boys for working hard. They prioritised sex, fighting and football as their areas of prowess. It is this group that has gained the most press attention. However, Mac an Ghaill identified further boys' subcultures in Parnell School. One was a group of white and Asian boys from skilled working-class backgrounds whom he called the **academic achievers**. They were in the top stream and spent much of their spare time in the drama department, partly to escape from the jibes of macho lads. Even some of the male teachers mocked them for their interest in 'feminine' subjects such as English and they felt inferior to more confident boys from middle-class backgrounds. However, they persisted in their studies, sometimes boosting their self-esteem through parodying gender issues.

Parminder: Sometimes you wonder if all the learning and study is worth it…You lose mates and you can't really get on with the snobs. I mean you wouldn't want to, would you?

MM: So what keeps you going?

Parminder: I like the work a lot of the time and I want to get on and that's what my family wants. I wouldn't want to be like the dossers here. My brother's like them. He's just wasting his life.

Quoted in M. Mac an Ghaill, *The Making of Men: Masculinities, Sexualities and Schooling* (1994)

The self-styled **real Englishmen** were a group of boys with professional parents. They were so confident about their cultural capital that they expected to succeed in school examinations with little effort. In any case, their parents' connections would sponsor them through university and into top jobs. They looked down on teachers, whom they regarded as low skilled 'guardians of mediocrity'.

Edward: Mark's the best when he starts arguing with the teachers. They start off talking down to him and then realise that he can defend himself. They get wickedly mad with him when he quotes some European philosopher they've never heard of. Then they're really shown up in front of everyone. And they hate that because that's their tactic with the kids.

Quoted in M. Mac an Ghaill, *The Making of Men: Masculinities, Sexualities and Schooling* (1994)

These observations undercut generalisations that middle-class students relate better to teachers than to working-class students and are more in tune with school aims. Another generalisation, that girls are better behaved and better motivated than boys, is also challenged by Mac an Ghaill. **The Posse** was a group of working-class white and black girls in the two lowest sets. They were a highly visible, badly behaved group regarded as a major challenge by teachers.

Linda: There's a lot of posses (gangs) in this school. A lot of boys are in them. But we are The Posse. The teachers have to check us out all the time. And even a lot of the boys are afraid of us…We live on the estate, went to the same primary school…When we came here, we just moved together and we got a reputation as a bad group. They put us all in the low classes, so that gives us more time together and we go round to each other's houses…People can't boss you around like they could if you are on your own…And it's just good because school is so boring. It's something to do and you look after each other.

Quoted in M. Mac an Ghaill, *The Making of Men: Masculinities, Sexualities and Schooling* (1994)

The girls' council estate had suffered mass deprivation as a result of high unemployment. It had a reputation for a high rate of violent crime and a large number of one-parent families. Their group identity was based on a strong sense of class solidarity.

'Masculine' teacher behaviour

The macho lads were usually taught by male teachers with confrontational styles. When female staff took these classes, their less controlling methods were not respected by the students, whose masculine codes had been reinforced by tough teachers.

In contrast, old collectivist male teachers tried to combat sexism but failed to realise they were guilty themselves. A female teacher described their behaviour:

When they talk about anti-sexist education, they're mainly talking in terms of changing the boys, the male pupils. Like they were active in stopping the boys playing football in the playground and taking up all the space. They see sexism as mainly a working-class problem. The liberals are much less aware of how they, as middle class men, take up space in more hidden ways…There has been a lot of sexual harassment from the male staff towards female teachers and pupils. Whether it's telling dirty jokes, sexual innuendoes, the leering looks or inappropriate touching.

Quoted in M. Mac an Ghaill, *The Making of Men: Masculinities, Sexualities and Schooling* (1994)

Another teacher observed:

Male teachers consistently try to dominate the agenda of any meetings; management and teaching is about male definitions of what is important. You see the crude ways in which male teachers will take up women's views at staff meetings and present them as their own.

Quoted in M. Mac an Ghaill, *The Making of Men: Masculinities, Sexualities and Schooling* (1994)

Mac an Ghaill suggests that, since the 1980s, 'the qualitative world of values' — the more caring side of school life, often associated with feminine and liberal ideals — has been eclipsed by the 'quantitative "masculine" world of the technology of change'. Government directives have encouraged schools to monitor and assess individual progress more regularly, which might be expected to produce closer staff–student relationships. However, the opposite occurred at Parnell School. The new entrepreneurs produced policy documents and quantitative methods of measuring individual progress that involved intensive staff training and record keeping but which reflected 'the conventional masculine splitting of rationality and emotions'. Staff busy with data collection had shallower relationships with students.

Pressure to be heterosexual

Mac an Ghaill finds fault with the wording of the Education Reform Act, which implies that the same curriculum will be relevant to all 'regardless of sex, ethnic origin and geographical location'. It ignores the fact that children from different backgrounds may have different experiences and needs. Likewise, he is critical of recent directives to promote conventional family life and heterosexuality in sex education lessons and to discourage alternative lifestyles. At Parnell School, homosexuality was rarely mentioned in lessons. Homosexual students told Mac an Ghaill that when literary texts by gay or lesbian authors were studied, their sexual orientation was not mentioned, so students gained no positive images, associating homosexuality primarily with AIDS. One of the school's outstanding footballers stopped playing because he was secretly gay and felt uncomfortable with the sport's celebration of powerful masculinity.

> You see they really fantasise about strength, posture and all that. And gays are supposed to be weak.
>
> Quoted in M. Mac an Ghaill, *The Making of Men: Masculinities, Sexualities and Schooling* (1994)

Homophobia was rife. When a boy, pleased with his examination results, gave Mac an Ghaill, who had taught him, a bunch of flowers in the playground, the boy swiftly became involved in a fight, and Mac an Ghaill was reprimanded by the head teacher for having apparently encouraged an inappropriate relationship. Mac an Ghaill suggests that 'heterosexuality is a highly fragile, socially constructed phenomenon' and that the cultures of the staffroom, classroom and playground create dominant heterosexual forms of masculinity that subordinate females and homosexuals. He quotes M. Lilley (1985):

Every teacher should be aware that any school where gay and lesbian staff and pupils are not made to feel relaxed and wholly open about their sexual orientation is one that is imposing a daily misery and injustice.

Lilley (1985), quoted in M. Mac an Ghaill, *The Making of Men: Masculinities, Sexualities and Schooling* (1994)

Task 3.3

Re-examine Mac an Ghaill's study and check whether the following generalisations are supported by his findings:

- Boys are less academically motivated than girls.
- In school, the behaviour of boys is worse than that of girls.
- Middle-class students relate better to teachers than do working-class students.
- Nowadays, teachers are aware of equal-opportunity issues.
- Vocational initiatives have been useful in enhancing students' prospects of gaining employment.
- Detailed tracking of progress benefits students.

David Jackson: changing equal opportunities teaching

Jackson reiterates Mac an Ghaill's concerns about links between the failure of boys and machismo. In an article in *Failing Boys?* (1998) he sets their behaviour in a context of disorientating social change.

> The old incentives, for many boys, to become respectable working men — status, pride, security — are now breaking apart. What some boys are left with is a bitter sense of the pointlessness of labour and an aggressive culture of heterosexual masculinity to fill in their despairing gaps.
>
> D. Jackson 'Breaking out of the binary trap', *Failing Boys?* (1998)

Since 1988, competition between schools has emphasised academic qualifications as never before, devaluing other kinds of knowledge and experience, such as familiarity with community languages. Raising levels of pupil achievement does not necessarily involve reducing educational inequality; more Afro-Caribbean and working-class boys are excluded by schools attempting to improve their results. Aggressive 'laddism' arises from lack of social justice.

Students have expressed resentment at the 'masculine' priority schools now give to results, their image in the community and their ability to attract business investment. What is needed is a return to a more holistic education where individuals matter. This could best be achieved by equal-opportunities work by all staff to change the gender culture in school. In a more caring atmosphere, boys could learn not to associate working hard with girls only and not to bully 'keenoes'. As their academic results improved, macho identities would not be required to boost their self-esteem. Girls' confidence would increase if they were no longer intimidated and harassed by male students and teachers. Jackson suggests some radical changes in attitudes.

Media images of manliness: Samuel L. Jackson in *The Man* and Russell Crowe in *Gladiator*

It also means critically investigating some boys' investments in media images of heroic manliness such as Arnold Schwarzenegger, Bruce Lee, Mel Gibson and Rambo. It means gendering the discussion and non-violent practices connected to boys' everyday aggression and bullying. Within the arena of boys' sexualities it means questioning heterosexual boys' attempts to score and feel powerful as a way of hiding their fears of failure…Challenging macho cultures can also mean noticing and changing how some boys use sexual harassment…to gain power over girls and other, sidelined boys. In terms of language, boys' verbal insults, jeering, name-calling, sexist jokes and put-downs also need to be explored and changed. The conformist pressures of the dominant peer group need to be critically exposed, particularly in the areas of sport and sex…And we need to examine closely the aggressive, militaristic culture which influences many boys through their videos, computer games and street-life culture…Many girls still lack confidence, often have low self-esteem and have limited educational and work aspirations. A positive action programme in schools still needs to work creatively on raising girls' low expectations.

D. Jackson 'Breaking out of the binary trap', *Failing Boys?* (1998)

Jackson suggests that many boys are currently damaging themselves and others through dominant forms of masculinity. Some are bewildered and confused and would secretly welcome 'public questioning of that taken-for-granted culture'.

Have the media misinterpreted gender-attainment patterns?

In *Failing Boys? Issues in Gender and Achievement* (1998), Debbie Epstein echoes many of the points discussed above and strikes a note of caution about the current moral panic over boys' 'failure'. She makes interesting observations, some of which could be used in essays to gain evaluation marks.

- Concerns over boys' 'idleness' and underachievements in education were recorded as early as 1963. Working class boys' resistance to schooling was documented by Paul Willis in 1977. Media suggestions that this is a new phenomenon are misleading. What is new is that girls have overtaken boys at A-level, which people with traditional views find surprising.
- Some boys are performing better than ever before.
- There are more attainment differences among boys and girls than between them. Social class is still a far more significant factor than gender, followed by school quality. Schools in the most deprived local education authorities come lowest in the league tables.
- There is a danger that concern over boys' progress, whipped up by men's movements, might result in schools being even more 'masculinised' than they already are. In a backlash against feminism, male writers, for example Robert Bly and Neil Lyndon, have aroused sympathy for 'poor boys, lost boys, damaged boys, under-fathered boys; boys at the mercy of feminist teachers'. Schemes such as making specifications and teaching methods more attractive to boys and arranging cadet corps, male mentoring and business links only for boys could counteract feminist initiatives.
- There should be more to education than results. The current marketisation of education puts undue emphasis on assessment and positions in league tables.
- School examination results do not automatically translate into economic advantage in employment. On average, males still earn more per hour than females.

Summary

- Girls' results are now better than boys' from Key Stage 1 to A-level and more girls than boys go to university. This is a change since the late 1980s, when girls began to overtake boys at A-level; by the mid-1990s a moral panic had begun about failing boys.

- Before then, sociologists tried to explain female underachievement. Explanations included:
  - patriarchal attitudes
  - socialisation
  - girls being steered into 'feminine' subjects and roles by the ideology of romance
  - teachers paying less attention to girls and allowing boys to dominate the classroom
  - a sexist hidden curriculum
- More recently, explanations of why girls have overtaken boys include:
  - greater opportunities for women as a result of feminism and changes in occupational structure
  - curriculum changes
  - equal opportunities initiatives in schools
- Boys' underachievement has been attributed to macho behaviour, particularly among working-class boys in response to the decline in manual employment.
- Different interests from an early age, such as a preference by boys for physical activities over reading, may be reinforced by parents, making it harder for boys to concentrate on literacy-related schoolwork.
- However, there is evidence that heterosexual masculinity still dominates many schools, resulting in the marginalisation of females and of boys perceived as lacking machismo. Wide-ranging, equal-opportunities initiatives are recommended to counteract macho views that schoolwork is for girls.
- New Labour's emphasis on measurable results, competition between schools and connections with business has been linked by some sociologists with oppressive heterosexual masculinity.
- The gap between male and female attainment has been overemphasised. Other factors, such as class differences, are more significant. Many girls still lack confidence and may opt for traditionally feminine jobs.

Task 3.4

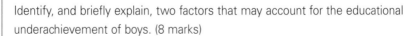

Identify, and briefly explain, two factors that may account for the educational underachievement of boys. (8 marks)

Guidance

- Before starting to write, ensure that you have selected two dissimilar reasons. Students often lose marks by describing in different words phenomena that are virtually the same.

Task 3.4 (continued)

- For each reason, start on a new line, perhaps marking it with a bullet point. Begin with a key word or phrase for the factor and then continue with a couple of sentences clarifying how this is likely to disadvantage males compared with females.

Task 3.5

Examine the reasons why females now tend to achieve more than males in the education system. (20 marks)

Guidance

As the question includes the word 'now', it is better to focus on factors that have recently changed, such as women's roles in wider society, making brief comparisons with the past.

There is so much information, that careful planning is needed. It might be useful to make notes under such headings as:

- parents and socialisation
- wider society and the job market
- teachers and the curriculum

Each set of factors could be discussed first in relation to girls' educational progress and then to that of boys.

To gain knowledge marks, you should include named studies and key vocabulary for each set of factors. Knowledge and understanding are the main focus in questions that begin with the word 'examine'.

A final paragraph, assessing the relative importance of the factors mentioned is likely to attract some of the evaluation marks available. In addition, make your essay more critical by identifying some of the disagreements between sociologists. Some of Epstein's comments, suggesting that female achievement has been overemphasised, could also be incorporated.

Research suggestions

- Replicate Sue Sharpe's *Just Like a Girl* by interviewing girls about their ambitions. As a comparison, ask older women about their teenage ambitions.
- Children's magazines, television programmes and toy promotions may still present sexist stereotypes. Investigate some of these, using either quantitative or interpretative methods.

Useful websites

- BBC News story: 'Boys 'fighting back' in A-levels'
  http://news.bbc.co.uk/1/hi/education/3577868.stm
- National Statistics Online — Education: 'Girls outperform boys at GCSE and A-level'
  www.statistics.gov.uk/cci/nugget.asp?id=434

Further reading

- Arnot, M. et al. (1999) *Closing the Gender Gap: Postwar Education and Social Change*, Polity Press.
- Clark, A. and Millard, E. (eds) (1998) *Gender in the Secondary Curriculum: Balancing the Books*, Routledge.
- Epstein, D. et al. (1998) *Failing Boys? Issues in Gender and Achievement*, Oxford University Press.

Does ethnicity influence educational attainment?

What are the patterns of ethnic minority attainment?

An **ethnic group** is one that sees itself as culturally distinct from other groupings in a society and is seen by others as distinctive. Such a group may differ from others in, for example, country of origin, language, religion, dress or other aspects of culture. Everyone belongs to an ethnic group, including white people whose ancestors have lived in Britain for as long as they can remember, so terms such as 'ethnics' are meaningless. Sociologists also avoid referring to different 'races', as there are disagreements about whether such groupings can be defined and the term has been used in derogatory ways.

Some ethnic groups, for example the Irish — Britain's largest ethnic minority — are not physically distinctive. Other more visible minorities may be subject to discrimination and harassment, including in the education system. Ever since the postwar influx of immigrants to Britain from the West Indies and the Indian subcontinent, sociologists and educationalists have been concerned about wide gaps in attainment between different ethnic groups. Why this occurs and the difficulties of reaching firm conclusions are the subjects of this chapter.

Table 4.1 Percentages of pupils in England achieving five or more grades A*–C at GCSE or GNVQ: by sex and ethnic group, 2004

Ethnic group	Boys	Girls
Chinese	70	79
Indian	62	72
White Irish	54	62
White British	47	57
Bangladeshi	41	55
Pakistani	38	52
Black African	37	48
Black Caribbean	27	44

Source: adapted from National Statistics Online

Table 4.1 shows the huge differences between the GCSE results of different ethnic groups in England, as well as striking gender differences. In 2004, Chinese pupils were the most likely to achieve five or more GCSE grades A*–C, with Indian pupils not far behind. Both groups outstripped white students, suggesting that their progress is not a cause for concern. On the other hand, two other south Asian groups performed less well and black Caribbean students, particularly boys, performed very poorly. This last group has been the greatest focus of concern in recent years, because low achievement in young males is associated with unemployment, antisocial behaviour and crime.

The relative positions of these groups have changed little since the Swann Report (1985) expressed concerns about male pupils of West Indian origin. Then, Bangladeshi pupils obtained the worst results, comparing badly with West Indians, a situation that has now changed. African-Asians performed exceptionally well.

How easy is it to compare groups?

The issue is complicated by social-class factors. Children of African-Asian backgrounds generally have middle-class, educated parents who enjoyed professional status in Africa before migrating. West Indian parents are more likely to be unemployed, so their children suffer from working-class disadvantage. Statistics that hold class constant, for example by comparing attainments of black and white children of middle-calss parents, show much smaller differences between the attainments of ethnic groups.

Other factors complicate the picture, as shown by Task 4.1.

Task 4.1

Read the following data, then answer the question that follows.

The Institute for Social and Economic Research's Labour Force Survey, published in 1995, found the following:

Members of all minority ethnic groups were more likely to stay on at school after the minimum leaving age than white teenagers. The proportion remaining in education was outstandingly high among African men and women — nearly three times as many were still at college at the age of 20, compared with whites. Indians also had high staying-on rates. Among the younger members of the sample, Caribbeans were rather more likely to continue in post-16 education than their white counterparts, but the difference was small, especially for boys, and had disappeared by the age of 20. Thus, young Caribbean men were at least as likely to continue their studies as white men, but were well behind some other minority groups in this respect.

Labour Force Survey, The Institute for Social and Economic Research (1995)

Task 4.1 (continued)

However, comparing the qualifications achieved by those who stayed on at each stage, Caribbean men required half a year longer, on average, in the education system to achieve the same qualifications as white men. African and Indian men required an additional year and Pakistani and Bangladeshi men an additional 2 years.

How do these data present a different picture of ethnic achievement from Table 4.1?

Guidance

- Notice that many ethnic minorities are ambitious to improve on the qualifications they achieved at 16.
- Qualifications obtained earlier or later than average are not shown in league tables.

Obtaining qualifications later than average may lose several years of earning power and make it harder to climb the occupational ladder. Do all ethnic groups eventually obtain similar qualifications? Box 4.1 shows how different groups have fared in achieving degrees.

Box 4.1

Higher qualifications by ethnic group

- In 2004, people from the Bangladeshi, black Caribbean and Pakistani groups were less likely than white British people to have a degree or equivalent.
- Among men, Bangladeshis and black Caribbeans were the least likely to have a degree (11% for each group).
- Among women, Bangladeshis and Pakistanis were the least likely to have a degree (5% and 10% respectively).
- The groups most likely to have degrees were Chinese (31%), Indian (25%) and white Irish (24%). These compared with 17% of white British people.

Source: adapted from National Statistics Online

The figures given in Box 4.1 include young people recently educated in British schools and colleges and older people, many of whom will have grown up abroad. The qualifications of those educated overseas tell us nothing about the success of our school system, but they are a useful indicator of the extent to which these adults may be able to help their school-age children, both academically and financially. The correlation with GCSE results is striking.

Why do some ethnic minorities underperform?

The types of explanation suggested for underperformance by some ethnic minorities have changed recently. Early studies tended to focus on psychological, cultural and material factors relating to the ethnic groups themselves. Many of these can loosely be called home factors. Some people felt that as ethnic minorities began to assimilate to life in Britain, their results would improve.

David Gillborn (1990) is one of several sociologists who have advocated a change of emphasis.

> Educationists speak of the underachievement of Afro-Caribbean pupils rather than the underachievement of the educational system.
>
> D. Gillborn, *Race, Ethnicity and Education: Teaching and Learning in Multi-Ethnic Schools* (1990)

In his view, school factors, particularly teachers' attitudes and aspects of the school curriculum, are more crucial explanations of different achievement patterns, though home factors, such as poverty, have some influence.

We shall begin with a brief survey of earlier explanations before examining in greater detail recent research offering explanations favoured today.

What 'home' factors have been linked with attainment?

Innate ability

Some psychologists, for example Hans Eysenck and Arthur Jensen, claimed that American black people had lower intelligence than white people. This was later discredited as the black students tested came from more disadvantaged backgrounds than the white students. The IQ tests set by white psychologists were likely to favour members of white cultures.

Language

Language differences may partly explain the lower educational attainments of some ethnic-minority children born abroad. Bangladeshis came to Britain relatively recently and at the time of the Swann Report were the lowest achieving group. Newly arrived black Caribbeans experienced difficulties in having their written work accepted, as their West Indian dialect (Creole) had significant grammatical differences from standard English. Bernard Coard (1971) suggested that white teachers often thought that such children were stupid because they failed to respond correctly to instructions. Unlike recent Asian immigrants, they were treated as English speakers, yet they often could not fully understand the teacher's form of English. However, children of Indian and Chinese origin are now among the highest achieving groups, suggesting that language problems affect only recent immigrants.

There is still some concern that children whose mother tongue is not English may have relatively restricted English vocabulary. However, their experience in coping with more than one language in their daily lives may be an advantage to them when learning new ones at school.

Family life

The Swann Report suggested that the more tightly knit Asian family structure, compared with the typical Afro-Caribbean one, might be responsible for higher levels of achievement in some Asian groups. Few women of southern Asian origin are single mothers, whereas the phenomenon is common among Afro-Caribbeans and increasingly so among whites.

Ken Pryce (1979) observed that Afro-Caribbean family life in Britain can be 'turbulent'. New Right commentators, such as Charles Murray, associate the children of never-married parents with underachievement and other forms of deviance. When mothers bring up children alone, often working as well, such children may receive inadequate parental stimulation and supervision, unless there is a support network of relatives or friends.

Task 4.2

Think of reasons (other than the lack of parental supervision) why the children of single parents might do less well at school.

Guidance
- Financial considerations might provide a clue.
- Why might such families be poorer?
- How does poverty affect educational success?

Families of immigrant origin appear to be more ambitious for their children than the white working class:
- According to Andrew Pilkington (1997), they are more likely to persuade children to stay on at school beyond 16.
- Ken Pryce (1979) found most of the Afro-Caribbean parents he interviewed in Bristol were keen for their children to progress academically.

- Ghazala Bhatti (1999) found the same for Asian parents.
- John Rex and Sally Tomlinson (1979) questioned the theory that southern Asian parents are keener on education than Afro-Caribbeans, finding that 10% more of the Afro-Caribbean parents than Asian parents interviewed had recently visited their children's school.

Task 4.3

Can you think of reasons (other than enthusiasm for education) why a higher proportion of Afro-Caribbean than Asian parents might visit their children's school?

Guidance

Consider the different types of work typically undertaken by these ethnic groups.

Material factors

There is ample research demonstrating the links between low parental income and children's educational disadvantage. In Britain, unemployment rates for non-whites are generally higher than for whites. In these days of dual income families, women's unemployment rates need to be considered as well as those of men. Examine the trends in Table 4.2.

Table 4.2 UK national unemployment, 2004

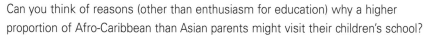

Male unemployment	Percentage
Black Caribbean, black African, Bangladeshi and mixed ethnic	13–14
Pakistani	11
Chinese	10
Indian	7
White British and Irish	6
Female unemployment	**Percentage**
Pakistani	20
Black African and mixed ethnic	12
Black Caribbean	9
Indian	8
Chinese	7
White British and Irish	4
Bangladeshi and Pakistani women were three times more likely to be economically inactive (not seeking paid work) than white British, Irish and black Caribbean women. Most were looking after their family or home.	

Which ethnic groups currently outperform whites in GCSEs, despite higher parental unemployment? This illustrates that no single factor can be held responsible for educational progress.

The relative poverty of many ethnic-minority parents means that their children are unlikely to attend independent schools, receive private tuition or have home computers. Bhatti (1999) found that, because of financial constraints, some Asian students left the education system sooner than their parents would have liked. Despite education maintenance allowances and university loans, low family income is a significant influence when contemplating post-16 education. This is particularly the case for single-income families, disproportionately affecting Afro-Caribbean children.

What school factors have been linked with attainment?

Ethnocentric curriculum

An ethnocentric curriculum denotes a school syllabus that reflects the dominant culture and ignores or marginalises the cultures of less influential ethnic groups. In 1971, Bernard Coard observed the absence of black literature, history and music in the British curriculum, and of positive images of black people in school books. He felt that this and the many negative associations of the word 'black' in the English language were likely to induce low self-esteem in Afro-Caribbean children and give them the feeling that school subjects had little relevance to their lives. The multicultural education movement attempted to address this by encouraging the teaching of world religions and the inclusion of black and Asian writers on literature syllabuses. However, since 1988, the national curriculum has reversed the trend by prescribing a large proportion of Christian teaching and the study of Shakespeare and pre-twentieth century authors.

Ethnic-minority groups have addressed this problem by setting up Saturday and supplementary schools to teach aspects of their own cultural heritage. Afro-Caribbeans in Slough organise additional weekend schooling where, as well as receiving individual help with work from mainstream school, students learn about West Indian and African culture and history. According to the organisers, the children's self-esteem, as well as their ability to cope academically, is boosted and the black teachers employed there provide useful role models of professional success. These ventures do not always receive government funding.

Overt racism

In 2000, the British Crime Survey found that 60% of Asian adults were worried about racially motivated attacks. This fear can also affect school attendance. Gillborn (1990) found that, at the comprehensive school he researched, racist name-calling by white students within school was an almost daily experience for Asian students. Physical attacks were also common and teachers responded inadequately. Several high-profile cases, such as the murder of Ahmed Iqbal Ullah, a 13-year-old Bangladeshi, in a Manchester school playground in 1986, indicate that this can be a serious problem. Asian students may respond to the threat by banding together for mutual protection, leading to accusations of keeping to themselves.

Ethnic-minority parents are less likely than white, middle-class parents to send their children to a better school some distance from home. Their local school tends to be preferred because it is in a familiar neighbourhood, perhaps making racial harassment less likely. They may also lack sufficient experience of the British education system to recognise the best-quality schools.

Institutional racism

Unlike the racism resulting from the prejudices of individuals, institutional racism is defined by the Commission for Racial Equality as the workings of organisations, rules and practices that have the effect of discriminating against particular ethnic groups.

Bernard Coard (1971) accused teachers of underestimating the abilities of Afro-Caribbeans, sending a high proportion to special schools and placing them in CSE rather than O-level streams. Before 1988, when league tables began to pressurise schools to obtain optimum results, there was evidence of teachers directing black students into sports and steel bands rather than academic study.

The Swann Report (1985) condemned the separate education in language centres of southern Asian children whose grasp of English was poor. The aim was to boost the English skills of new immigrants in about a year of intensive study, so that they could cope better in mainstream schools. However, separate education in small centres meant that they were denied access to the full range of educational facilities available to other students. This example shows that good intentions in education may produce negative effects.

More recently, Gillborn and Youdell (2000) noted that a disproportionate number of black students in the schools they studied were entered for foundation tiers in GCSEs, meaning that they could only achieve, at best, C grades. Therefore, they would be unlikely to progress to A-levels. The decisions about entering students for GCSEs were based on teachers' estimates of the students' ability and might have been influenced by stereotyping, such as the view that Afro-Caribbean boys are anti-school. Further details are given in Box 4.2.

Box 4.2

A consistent finding, in both the US and the UK, is that where education systems use some form of internal differentiation (through tracking, setting, banding, streaming), black pupils are usually overrepresented in the lower status groups. These groups typically receive poorer resources and are often taught by less experienced (and/or less successful) teachers. Of course, these lower ranked groups are not overtly determined on the basis of ethnic origin — they are usually presented as a reflection of the pupils' capabilities, that is, their 'ability'. But...we should be incredibly cautious and critical whenever we are told that certain pupils (disproportionately black pupils) are less able, less well developed, or whatever is the preferred phrase of the moment to describe those pupils who have been deemed to be outside the chosen ranks of those destined to succeed. We need this caution because, despite the façade of value-neutral standardised testing and teachers' 'professional judgement', in school the word 'ability' is very often another word for what teachers think/assume children can do...Even leading researchers in intelligence testing...now agree that tests cannot measure innate potential.

D. Gillborn, 'It takes a nation of millions (and a particular kind of education system) to hold us back', in Richardson, B. (ed.) *Tell it Like it is: How our Schools Fail Black Children* (2005)

Recent opinion: teacher attitudes and student responses

Recent research has attributed attainment differences between ethnic groups to variations in teacher attitudes to different groups, combined with student responses to apparently unfair treatment. This is primarily a school factor as it involves classroom interaction. However, teachers may be responding to media stereotypes of black youths as criminals, 'gangsta rappers' or at least a 'problem', and young people sometimes reinforce this by celebrating street styles in school. In addition, the unemployment and discrimination suffered by some groups inevitably affect their attitudes to education. The studies that follow show that attempting to categorise influences into home and school factors is scarcely feasible.

Cecile Wright: 'them and us'

Cecile Wright interviewed teachers and groups of Year 10 students in two Midland comprehensives in 1986. Both schools had previously been grammar schools and older teachers tended to associate the more challenging teaching conditions with the influx of high proportions of ethnic-minority students. One said that 'English culture is being swamped'. Staffroom comments about Afro-Caribbean students as troublemakers meant that new teachers met them with stereotypes already formed and tended to punish them more harshly than white students for similar behaviour. Some teachers made insensitive jokes that black pupils found disrespectful. In response to this 'hassle', students formed anti-school subcultures. A student told Wright, 'If the teachers have no respect for you, there's no way I'm going to respect them'.

In one school, 'gangs' of black boys asserted themselves by speaking patois, which made the teachers feel threatened and resulted in a 'them-and-us' atmosphere.

Professor Cecile Wright

Wright concluded:

> If pupils discern a repeated pattern of injustice, discontent may well become general among the pupils affected and come to have a lowering effect on the whole life and work of the school.

Education for Some (1986)

Use Task 4.4 to assess Foster's criticisms of Wright's study.

Task 4.4

Read the passage and answer the questions that follow.

In 1991, Peter Foster published an article entitled 'Case not proven', challenging the validity of Wright's study of teacher racism in two schools. He pointed out that Wright provided no first-hand evidence of teacher racism. She simply quoted

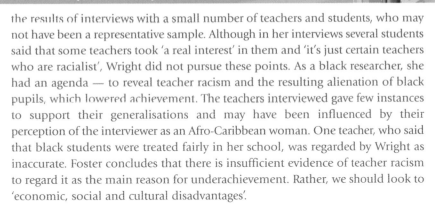

Task 4.4 (continued)

the results of interviews with a small number of teachers and students, who may not have been a representative sample. Although in her interviews several students said that some teachers took 'a real interest' in them and 'it's just certain teachers who are racialist', Wright did not pursue these points. As a black researcher, she had an agenda — to reveal teacher racism and the resulting alienation of black pupils, which lowered achievement. The teachers interviewed gave few instances to support their generalisations and may have been influenced by their perception of the interviewer as an Afro-Caribbean woman. One teacher, who said that black students were treated fairly in her school, was regarded by Wright as inaccurate. Foster concludes that there is insufficient evidence of teacher racism to regard it as the main reason for underachievement. Rather, we should look to 'economic, social and cultural disadvantages'.

According to Foster, what criticisms could be made of:

- Wright's sample?
- her selectivity when interviewing?
- the teachers' evidence?
- how interviewer effect may have operated?

If Wright had been a white researcher, would this have solved the problems of bias and having an agenda?

Guidance

- Samples need to be large and carefully selected in order to reflect a typical range of opinions.
- Interviewers should avoid directing respondents towards certain responses, yet they need to probe enough to gain detailed evidence.
- Inevitably, the characteristics of the interviewer may influence the responses obtained.

Mairtin Mac an Ghaill: problems of researcher identity

In contrast to Wright, Mairtin Mac an Ghaill, an Irish sociologist, described in *Beyond the White Norm* (1989) his own early research into education and ethnicity as being too much from a white standpoint:

> When I began to examine the schooling of black young people, I did not initially report their view of things.
>
> M. Mac an Ghaill, *Beyond the White Norm* (1989)

He criticised other researchers for their 'culturalist perspective', adopting the 'white norm' of viewing the black community as a 'problem'. An example is to contrast the 'pathological' Afro-Caribbean family structure with the assumed unity of the Asian extended-family network.

For his study at 'Kilby School', Mac an Ghaill used the black sociologist Paul Gilroy, a 'soul head', as a 'gatekeeper' to help him gain an insider view of Afro-Caribbean youths' informal social divisions into funk heads, soul heads and Rasta heads. Mac an Ghaill taught at the school, observed other teachers and interviewed teachers, students and their parents. He opened his house to students in their leisure time to deepen his insight into their experiences. He concluded that, while well-meaning teachers thought that they treated all students the same, ethnic-minority students received unfair treatment, which led to resentment. Adding to their general awareness of racial and social-class disadvantages outside school, this led some Afro-Caribbean and Asian males to form anti-school subcultures. Such behaviour boosted their morale but was damaging to their school progress.

In contrast, a group he called the 'black sisters' resented the white bias of the school history curriculum but accommodated to it in order to succeed, 'so that we can tell them that black people are not stupid'. Students described Mac an Ghaill as 'Irish, not white', which helped him to be accepted. However, there were some topics that the black sisters probably kept from him. One of them said:

> You can't really know what it's like for a black woman. That's why I think that although what you have done is good, I think that black women should carry out their own studies.

> Quoted in M. Mac an Ghaill, *Beyond the White Norm* (1989)

David Gillborn: avoiding confrontations

Gillborn's observations (1990) over 2 years at 'City Road' comprehensive confirm the views of Wright and Mac an Ghaill that secondary-school age Afro-Caribbean boys may be viewed as a threat to teachers' authority. He found that they were reprimanded far more than white or Asian students for the same offence — for example, being singled out for chatting in class when most pupils were doing so. In addition, Gillborn used a quantitative method of comparing reasons why students of different ethnic groups were entered in the school's detention books. He found that while pupils of other ethnicities were more often punished for breaking school rules, a disproportionate number of Afro-Caribbean students had received detentions for 'offences whose identification rested primarily in the teachers' interpretation of pupil attitude or intent'. Their behaviour was frequently viewed as a challenge to authority, even though no regulation had been broken.

White teachers often tried to repress Caribbean cultural differences, such as features of dress and speech, reading them as strategies of resistance. This control extended even to behaviour with no bearing on educational progress — for example, boys were reprimanded for a particular style of walking. In contrast, the cultural differences exhibited by Asians were not perceived as threatening. They were treated in the classroom with the same discipline as white students, so were often able to fulfil their potential.

Gillborn paid close attention to the interaction of particular individuals with teachers. The most common response of Afro-Caribbean boys to continued unfair treatment was to be drawn together in increasing opposition to the school. In the resulting anti-school subcultures, 'clique members revelled in their ethnicity and physical prowess, and would respond angrily to occasions where they felt themselves to be treated unfairly'.

Such confrontations sometimes led to expulsion. More often, badly behaved students were contained in small groups not destined for examinations.

Unfortunately, the high rate of Afro-Caribbean expulsions was not confined to 'City Road' comprehensive; the UK government is now so concerned, that schools have to record the ethnicity of every student they expel. The problem is outlined in Box 4.3.

Box 4.3

School exclusions

In England in 2003–04, pupils from black Caribbean, other black and mixed white and black Caribbean groups were among the most likely to be permanently excluded from schools. Black Caribbean rates were 41 per 10 000 — almost three times the rate for white pupils (14 per 10 000). Chinese and Indian pupils had the lowest exclusion rates (2 or less per 10 000).

Source: National Statistics Online

Gillborn did track a few highly motivated black students who, in contrast to the rebels at 'City Road', did all they could to avoid confrontations with teachers, apologising even when scarcely at fault. This was the case with the student Paul Dixon, which is described in Box 4.4

Gillborn's detailed ethnographic study demonstrates empathy for ethnic minority students; they were willing to confide in him despite his identity as a white researcher.

> **Box 4.4**
> **Paul Dixon**
>
> Paul did not emphasise his ethnicity through any displays of dress or demeanour, for instance, in styles of walking or speech...Paul distanced himself not only from certain members of staff but also from some of his closest friends within the school...Paul Dixon recognised and rejected the negative image that some staff held of him. Rather than reacting through a glorification of that image within a culture of resistance, however, Paul channelled his energies into succeeding against the odds by avoiding trouble when he could and minimising the conflicts which he experienced with his teachers ...Paul Dixon's case illustrated the very great demands which academically ambitious Afro-Caribbean pupils must meet if they are to succeed despite teacher ethnocentrism: 'mere' ability and dedication to hard work are not enough, they must also adapt to their disadvantaged position in such a way that they do not reinforce the widespread belief that they represent a threat to the teachers' authority.
>
> Adapted from D. Gillborn, *Race, Ethnicity and Education: Teaching and Learning in Multi-Ethnic Schools* (1990)

Tony Sewell: black teachers' responses

Black sociologist Tony Sewell claimed that being older but of the same ethnic background as the Afro-Caribbean boys he studied gave him 'critical distance' but 'affinity'. In *Black Masculinities and Schooling: How Black Boys Survive Modern Schooling* (1997), he wrote about a preliminary study that he conducted at the co-educational comprehensive 'John Caxton School' in an area of high unemployment. Afro-Caribbean boys made up one-third of the school population but 85% of the exclusions. Although teachers saw themselves as progressive and were not racist in the usual sense, they displayed more control and negative criticism of Afro-Caribbean boys. They tended to explain problems of interaction in terms of the boys' subcultural background and home, rather than identifying any fault within the school or with individual teachers. Even black teachers blamed black youth culture as a disruptive force in the school.

Some black students, ambitious for success, distanced themselves from the anti-school subculture by adopting a raceless persona, avoiding street fashions and befriending students from other cultures, which earned them the label 'battymen' (homosexuals). Nevertheless, they were still disproportionately excluded by the school, their actions being misinterpreted and punished more harshly than those of white students. These black students paid the high price of peer-group hostility, without avoiding negative discipline from teachers.

Task 4.5

- Compare Sewell's comment about his 'critical distance' but 'affinity' with Foster's comments on Wright's study and Mac an Ghaill's assessment of his own research position. Why is researcher identity such a problem for this topic?
- Could similar problems arise for sociologists studying class or gender?
- What do Gillborn's case study of Paul Dixon and Sewell's references to black students with a 'raceless persona' have in common?
- When you have read Chapter 5, consider these studies from the perspective of labelling.

Guidance

Consult textbooks about research methods to clarify concepts such as interviewer effect, interviewer bias and value freedom.

After his time at John Caxton School, Sewell made a detailed ethnographic study of 'Township School', a boys' comprehensive with about one-third Afro-Caribbean students. He conducted semi-structured interviews with teachers and students individually and in groups, and carried out daily observations in the playground and common rooms, 'chilling out' with the students.

Most teachers at Township were preoccupied with their own survival in a challenging school and they emphasised the need to control the students and exclude troublemakers. Even though there was evidence of unfairness and over-reaction by some teachers, few considered that their own practice involved racist stereotyping, a situation that increased student disaffection. Some teachers feared the large physique of Afro-Caribbean students. They tended to blame a lack of responsible fathering for perceived bad behaviour by black students.

While uninterested white students truanted from school and had, on average, achieved worse examination results, reluctant black students still attended, because they were more likely to be stopped by the police if found on the streets. This meant that a higher proportion of disaffected black students had confrontations with teachers.

Sewell acknowledged that many black students were rebels. He related their behaviour to Merton's strain theory (1938). Afro-Caribbeans shared other students' goals of success but felt unlikely to achieve them by legitimate means because the odds were stacked against them. This led to deviant responses.

Other boys accepted the need for education, emphasised by ambitious Caribbean parents, yet rejected the day-to-day discipline of school and were in frequent confrontations with staff. They were torn between the pro-education values of their parents and the macho subculture that regarded education as feminised.

Unexpectedly, the fact that the headmaster of the school was black seemed to make matters worse. His main mission was to produce respectable-looking black students who would be acceptable to the labour market, so he had strict rules against black hairstyles with patterns, yet tolerated white-youth styles such as ponytails. As a result, black students were more often excluded for flouting school rules.

Older teachers from the Caribbean may have a traditional hard-work ethic and an intense dislike of current British black street culture. Increasing the proportion of black teachers is not an easy solution.

Why is researching ethnicity and education difficult?

The research above demonstrates that linking ethnicity and educational attainment is complex because:
- so many ethnic groups are involved
- class and gender differences complicate attempts to interpret statistics
- patterns of school achievement are misleading for groups that acquire qualifications later in life
- many different home, school and cultural factors interact
- the ethnicity and other characteristics of researchers may affect their conclusions
- findings in this ethically sensitive area may be influenced by political correctness

Current thinking tends to focus on teacher–pupil interaction as one of the main reasons for differences in attainment between groups, with home factors, such as poverty, also playing a significant part.

Summary

- Results in school examinations differ dramatically between ethnic groups, although there is some closing of the gap through post-school courses.
- Language differences, family structures and parental poverty are among the home factors that some sociologists consider responsible for the poorer school results of some ethnic groups.

- School factors include the ethnocentric curriculum, overt racism and institutional racism.
- Recent studies suggest that even well-meaning teachers may be influenced by stereotypes of disruptive Afro-Caribbean and diligent Asian students and consequently treat them differently. This often leads to confrontations with Afro-Caribbeans, the formation of anti-school subcultures and a disproportionately high rate of expulsions.
- Research in this area is complicated by other factors, such as class and gender, and the ethnic identity of the researcher.

Task 4.6

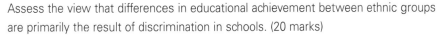

Assess the view that differences in educational achievement between ethnic groups are primarily the result of discrimination in schools. (20 marks)

Guidance
Knowledge and application
Research the different types of discrimination before you begin this essay, and seek studies as examples.

- **Prejudice** is a learned bias for or against members of particular groups, whereas discrimination is action based on such an attitude.
- **Discrimination** is usually used to denote unfavourable treatment of people assigned to a particular category:
  - **Direct discrimination** involves deliberately treating groups differently — for example, by the overt racism of taunts and attacks or the sometimes well-intentioned establishment of different schools for different ethnic groups.
  - **Indirect discrimination** may be unintentional. Imposing a school uniform that does not allow turbans or arranging a field trip that clashes with, for example, an important Jewish festival makes life harder for students from some cultural backgrounds. The **ethnocentric curriculum** might also be viewed as unintentionally discriminatory.
- More difficult to categorise is the sort of behaviour Geoffrey Driver (1984) observed. Teachers did not have the 'cultural competence' to realise that West Indian pupils who looked away while being reprimanded might be doing so out of respect, not as a sign of indifference.
- **Cultural or new racism** involves holding a cluster of views about the abilities and attributes of an ethnic group, such as supposing that Asians like studying and that Afro-Caribbeans prefer macho street culture. Gillborn found evidence of this.
- **Institutional racism** involves systematic discrimination, such as frequently assigning some ethnic minorities to lower GCSE tiers.

Task 4.6 (continued)

Evaluation

- There is plenty of research evidence of these types of discrimination, but remember to evaluate the studies. Some might be quite dated or use methods that you could query.
- Assessment also means pointing out agreement and disagreement between different studies.
- A section of your essay should refer to the possibility that differences in educational achievement between ethnic groups might not be primarily due to discrimination but perhaps a result of poverty, family structures or other home factors. You should give some evidence in support.

Conclusion

Finally, decide whether or not you consider discrimination to be the main cause of differences in attainment. If you think it is, you could perhaps restate the types of discrimination that you think are the most crucial. If necessary, analyse why it is difficult to reach a conclusion.

Task 4.7

Some of the possible reasons for social-class, ethnic-minority and boys' or girls' educational underachievement are similar. Sometimes questions expect you to refer to several of these areas by asking about the attainment of 'different social groups' or students of 'different home backgrounds'.

Divide a piece of paper into three columns and list similar reasons for class, ethnic and gender disadvantage next to each other — for example, material factors and language use. Add the names of researchers to provide yourself with a really useful revision aid.

Research suggestions

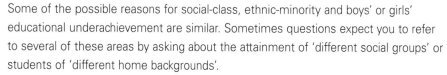

- Investigate a sample of the specifications and teaching materials at your school or college to see if they appear ethnocentric. Seek guidance from staff and the opinions of ethnic-minority students. Alternatively, visit a primary school to assess the readers in use and ask whether the children study the festivals of ethnic-minority religions.
- Interviews with ethnic-minority students about their experiences in education would be another interesting way of testing some of the theories above. Careful pre-planning of questions is needed for exploration of such a sensitive area.

- If there are supplementary schools for ethnic-minority groups in your area, you might be able to write a case study of one or two, providing that you can gain access and that you follow ethical guidelines.

Useful websites

- National Statistics Online — click on education, and training
  www.statistics.gov.uk/
- Article on social inequalities in education, with charts
  www.statistics.gov.uk/downloads/theme_compendia/fosi2004/Education.pdf
- Aiming High: Raising the Achievement of Minority Ethnic Pupils, DfES document
  www.standards.dfes.gov.uk/local/midbins/ema/Aiming_High_Consultation_Doc.DOC

Further reading

- Gillborn, D. (1990) *Race, Ethnicity and Education: Teaching and Learning in Multi-Ethnic Schools*, Unwin Hyman.
- Richardson, B. (ed.) (2005) *Tell it Like it is: How our Schools Fail Black Children*, Bookmarks Publications and Trentham Books.

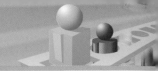

How do processes within schools influence attainment?

How do interactionists study education?

Interviews with secondary school students, conducted by Martin Bashir for BBC2's *Just One Chance* programme in 1998, provided insight into classroom relationships:

'What is it about a teacher,' asks Bashir, 'that makes you decide you want to challenge them — take them on?'

A girl answers: 'There's some teachers which you can just look at, and tell, and there's others which you just don't know about — so you try.'

'It's body language,' someone suggests.

'And if they're confident with their class,' the girl goes on, 'like if they're not sure whether to approach you or stuff like that.'

BBC2, *Just One Chance*, 1998

The evidence would interest interactionists — sociologists whose methods involve studying closely the way people interpret each other's actions and react to them. Some interactionists feel that working-class children and other groups are less successful at school because they arrive with negative attitudes to education; others focus on teachers' prior expectations of students. Most interaction involves language, based on a set of symbols, so this approach is sometimes called symbolic interactionism. Small-scale classroom studies often involve observing how students and teachers change their behaviour in response to each other and interviewing them about the experiences.

Do teachers label students?

People categorise each other very quickly, often based on superficial evidence. In Chapter 4, we saw how Gillborn, Wright and Sewell described teachers' expectations of different ethnic groups. When Howard Becker interviewed Chicago school teachers in the 1950s he found that one of their major problems was knowing how to deal with working-class pupils.

> They don't have the right kind of study habits. They can't seem to apply themselves as well. Of course, it's not their fault: they aren't brought up right. After all, the parents in a neighbourhood like that really aren't interested.
> H. Becker (1952) 'Social Class Variations in the Teacher–Pupil Relationship', *Journal of Educational Psychology*, Vol. 25, No. 6, pp. 45–65.

The teachers' preconceived ideas of class differences meant that social characteristics of whole groups of students, such as speech, dress and body language, were often taken to indicate lack of motivation and ability, so they were given less demanding work. The teachers and their managers expected the achievements of such groups to be lower than average, with the result that, over time, the gap between their attainment and that of middle-class children became greater. Dividing students into 'ability groups' affected their futures. For example, they might be entered for lower exam tiers or directed towards less academic courses.

The self-fulfilling prophecy

Another effect of labelling is the altered self-concept, called by Cooley the looking-glass self. If students sense that teachers have low expectations of their ability, they often believe this and view themselves as failures. They might stop trying. Conversely, if high teacher expectations are picked up by pupils, they might improve their performance.

This was illustrated by an American experiment carried out by R. Rosenthal and L. Jacobson known as *Pygmalion in the Classroom* (1968). Teachers were told that particular children were likely to make rapid progress. In fact, the children were chosen at random and IQ tests showed that they were no more able than the control group. However, after a year, further tests revealed that these students achieved higher scores than the others. The teachers had probably taken extra interest in them, believing them to be brighter, so their confidence and motivation were boosted.

Rosenthal and Jacobson's experiment suggests that once children are the subject of expectations and perceive this, what the teachers expect of them is likely to follow. This phenomenon is known as the self-fulfilling prophecy. Merton (1957) explains the phenomenon as follows:

> The self-fulfilling prophecy is, in the beginning, a 'false' definition of a situation evoking a new behaviour which makes the originally false conception come 'true'. This specious validity of the self-fulfilling prophecy perpetuates a reign of error. For the prophet will cite the actual course of events as proof that he was right from the beginning.
>
> R. K. Merton, *Social Theory and Social Structure* (1949)

Task 5.1

Discuss the following questions:

(a) Experiments in sociology are fairly rare. How does an experiment differ from a classroom observation such as Gillborn's at 'City Road' comprehensive? Some experiments have been criticised as unethical. Do you think this applies to Rosenthal and Jacobson's?

(b) Are people always affected in the same way by others' views of them?

Guidance

(a) Ethical guidelines for research include avoiding deception and not causing participants any harm.

(b) Remind yourself of Mac an Ghaill's study of the 'black sisters' and Gillborn's description of the student Paul Dixon. Look up Margaret Fuller's 1984 study of black girls in a London comprehensive.

Other labelling studies

There is evidence of labelling at every stage in the school career. Ray Rist (1970) noted how, in the absence of test information, a black kindergarten teacher divided black children into reading groups based on her own observations of their social characteristics. They were assigned to the 'fast readers' table' if they appeared clean, smartly dressed and interested, spoke with less dialect, were at ease with adults and came from homes with middle-class qualities. The teacher interacted more with the fast readers, whose table was at the front of the classroom and she praised them frequently. Students on the 'slower tables' further back in the room received less stimulation and more reproofs. Any gap in real ability between the groups was likely to widen over the year as a result of the differentiated treatment they received, all based on the teacher's initial categorisation. Though this may have been rather an extreme case, other researchers have found similar evidence of social and ethnic background influencing grouping and subsequent progress.

Aaron Cicourel and John Kitsuse (1971) studied 'typing' or stereotyping by counsellors in American high schools, who decided which students should be placed on courses that prepared for college entry. Their recommendations were based not only on grades but also on observations of demeanour, clothing, hairstyle, manner of speech and conduct reports. Students of high social class were placed on higher-level courses than those with similar academic records but lower class origins.

Patrick Shannon (1992) conjectures that teachers expect less academic success from working-class children because most share the popular view that 'lower-class people possess intellectual and character flaws that account for their lack of previous success and inhibit their prospects in the future, and that middle-class and upper-class people are successful because they are industrious and resourceful'.

Arguments for and against labelling theory are given in Table 5.1.

| Table 5.1 | Evaluation of labelling theory |

Arguments against labelling theory	Arguments supporting labelling theory
'There's no smoke without fire'. If teachers label working-class or similar groups of children as more likely to fail, it may be based on years of experience of exactly that.	There may be many reasons why certain groups underperform. If labelling can be minimised, students and their teachers will have more chance of combating other problems.
Labelling studies pay little attention to why some groups are negatively labelled; they ignore the power structures of society.	Interactionists do not claim that labelling theory alone explains everything. Some, such as Stuart Hall, are also Marxists.
Labelling theory is too deterministic; it assumes that everyone will be affected in the same way. In practice, some students ignore labels and others challenge them. Margaret Fuller found that a group of black London schoolgirls resented teachers' expectations of poor performance and worked hard to prove them wrong.	Labelling studies are less deterministic than critics suggest. The authors have never suggested that all students conform to labels or that this is the only reason students fail. Gillborn, Mac an Ghaill and Sewell all described students who resisted teacher labelling. Nevertheless, labelling increased the problems these students experienced in their school careers.
Many teachers have studied the sociology of education and are familiar with inter-actionist research, so they are now less likely to label students.	Though some of the most famous labelling studies were conducted in the 1970s, recent research suggests stereotyping still occurs, especially of some ethnic minorities.

Arguments against labelling theory	Arguments supporting labelling theory
Labelling studies usually involve observation of just one class or, at most, several classes at one school. The samples may not be representative of classroom situations nationwide.	There are a large number of British and American labelling studies providing corroborative evidence. They relate to a wide range of age groups, ethnic groups, social classes, girls and boys at various types of schools, providing a full picture in spite of small samples.
Labelling studies are usually qualitative and, therefore, subjective. The conclusions are often based on interpretation by one researcher.	Most labelling studies are based on detailed classroom observation over a long period and findings are often enhanced by in-depth interviews. They provide more thorough empirical evidence than studies in many other areas.
Today, most schools have equal opportunities and inclusion policies.	Recent evidence from Gillborn suggests that teachers who believe in equal opportunities often treat students differently, without realising this. Their expectations of certain social groups are unconsciously held, undermining sincere efforts to do their jobs well.
Schools are under pressure to gain good league table results, so teachers will be unwilling to label any students as failures.	League table concerns may lead to the expulsion of students who have been labelled as disruptive.

Does streaming affect progress?

Though many British state schools have a comprehensive intake, most divide students according to 'ability' so that individuals can work alongside those thought capable of progressing at a similar pace. This may be carried out by grouping students into broad bands, supposedly based on their general ability; the students study all subjects in those bands. An alternative method is to stream or set students for each subject separately, so they might be in different streams for different subjects.

Though these procedures sound sensible, sociological evidence shows that, once children are divided into different ability groups, the gap between the groups widens. This may be attributable both to teacher labelling and to the formation of anti-school subcultures within lower groups. The situation is particularly regrettable if banding and streaming are not based on real ability but on teacher expectations, linked to such factors as class or ethnicity.

There are various reasons why students placed in lower ability groups fail to progress. These include:

- low academic expectations by well-meaning teachers, who may set easier work and less homework than the group could manage
- lessons likely to contain less of the higher-level knowledge valued by examiners and more time-filling practical activities, such as copying and colouring
- less effort by teachers who resent having to teach 'weaker' students
- students being entered for fewer examination subjects and at lower levels
- individual students experiencing lowered self-esteem and reduced motivation (the self-fulfilling prophecy)
- disillusioned students forming anti-school subcultures and distracting each other, so that there is peer group pressure to underperform
- teachers tolerating more noise and poorer behaviour to avoid confrontation

Nell Keddie, Michael Young and the differentiated curriculum

In 1973, Nell Keddie observed humanities lessons in a comprehensive school and noted a hierarchy in the content of subjects taught to different streams. The upper streams, containing more middle-class students, received academic knowledge needed for examinations. Lower streams, predominantly working class, received a watered-down syllabus, with more practical activities to keep them occupied but less of the knowledge valued by examiners. They were permitted to make more noise, were set less homework and soon picked up the message that staff expectations of them were low.

Michael Young, in *Knowledge and Control* (1971) relates this situation to the fact that members of dominant groups regard their sort of knowledge as valuable and wish to ensure that it is only passed down to selected people of the same social level, to safeguard their positions in society:

> Increasing differentiation is a necessary condition for some groups to be in a position to legitimise their knowledge as superior or of high value. This high value is institutionalised by the creation of formal educational establishments to 'transmit' it to specially selected members of the society. Highly valued knowledge becomes enshrined in the academy or school and provides a standard against which all else that is known is compared.
>
> M. Young, *Knowledge and Control* (1971)

Even though we now have a national curriculum, there is still huge variation in the number of GCSE subjects taken by students. Also, there are short and full-length GCSEs, different tiers and vocational qualifications. Higher levels of

knowledge are less available to many students and, according to Young, this deprives them of power in the long run.

David Hargreaves: how streaming causes polarisation

In an influential study, *Social Relations in a Secondary School* (1967), David Hargreaves compared two streams of boys in a secondary modern school. He found that selection for the streams related more closely to behaviour than to ability. Those in the higher stream felt rewarded and they became even more conformist, attending and achieving well. The lower-stream boys felt unable to achieve high status in the teachers' eyes. Instead, they sought an alternative form of status among their peer group by being tough and daring. They formed an anti-school subculture that promoted 'delinquescent' behaviour.

Procedures within the school increased polarisation of the 'ability' groups. More effective teachers were assigned to the top streams; less experienced or weaker staff struggled with problem students, often resulting in classroom chaos. In order to encourage achievement in the top streams, teachers emphasised their superiority with comments such as:

> You're the only form in the school I can trust. I wouldn't dare let 4E do a job like this. They'd make a complete mess of it.
>
> Quoted in D. Hargreaves, *Social Relations in a Secondary School* (1967)

They also discouraged friendship across ability groups.

> I tell him to go round with lads in his own form. 'They're not for you,' I tell him.
>
> Quoted in D. Hargreaves, *Social Relations in a Secondary School* (1967)

The result was that boys in the lower streams began to regard members of higher streams as snobs and were likely to reject both them and all academic values. Once students in the lower-ability streams formed anti-school subcultures, it was difficult for the teacher to encourage pro-school behaviour from the few academically orientated members of the class — praising them would stress their difference from the rest. Teacher approval was likely to encourage these students to be more disruptive in order to retain some status in the peer group.

On a daily basis, subcultural acceptance is more rewarding to students than occasional praise from the teacher. According to Hargreaves, the problems can only be solved by charismatic teachers winning the loyalty of the informal leaders of the subculture. As this rarely occurs, the complete abolition of streaming is a more effective solution.

Peter Woods: complex adaptations to streaming

In 1979, Peter Woods conducted an ethnographic study of a mixed secondary modern school, observing lessons and interviewing students and staff. In *The Divided School*, he broadly agreed with Hargreaves that students fell into two groups — conformist and dissonant — and that this was emphasised after subject choices at the end of what is now Year 9.

For students in the top streams, mostly middle class, subject choice was a positive experience because, encouraged by parents and within-group pressure, they saw society as a contest system in which they had a chance of success. Few parents of lower-stream students, who were more likely to be working class, attended the headmaster's talk giving advice about subject choices. Their children chose non-examination subjects arbitrarily and so were alienated from the school's processes that some even forgot what they had chosen.

However, Woods painted a more complex picture than Hargreaves. He noted that at various points in their school careers, many students oscillated between conformity and dissonance and differed in their behaviour depending on the subject and the member of staff.

> Teachers vary in their methods, which they are at quite some liberty to do in the autonomy of their classrooms, and pupils vary in their responses. To give an obvious example, a pupil might reject formal methods, and accept informal ones. In short, there needs to be some recognition in the model of variations in individual pupils' responses.
>
> P. Woods, *The Divided School* (1979)

Types of conformity include:
- 'teacher's pets' who ingratiate themselves and become unpopular with their peers
- keen students who identify with the goals of the school
- ritualists who are not motivated, but behave within the norms of the school

> *PW*: What sort of pupil would you say you were?
>
> *Derek*: Pretty average really. I do me work. I behave meself.
>
> *PW*: What do you hope to get out of it?
>
> *Derek*: Dunno really. I just do what I'm told.
>
> *PW*: What do you come to school for?
>
> *Derek*: Well you have to, don't you. Ain't got much choice.'
>
> Quoted in P. Woods, *The Divided School* (1979)

In contrast, Woods describes:
- intransigent students, who deliberately disrupt lessons and even assault staff

- colonisers — students who work the system in order to survive, sometimes breaking rules, sometimes not
- rebellious students, who are less confrontational, but reject school tasks in favour of gossiping and practices such as doing their hair

> At times, colonisers might use illegal means, or 'short cuts' at least, such as copying someone else's homework, cribbing in tests and examinations or lying to avoid punishments…Volunteering for one job might avoid a more onerous one…playing off one teacher against another is common, or parents against teachers, such as in the endless stream of notes some bring to excuse them from games.
>
> Rebellious students can sometimes be persuaded to take an interest in particular lessons that strike them as relevant, such as ones on childcare.
>
> P. Woods, The Divided School (1979)

Woods observes that, although students pursuing the school's more academic courses are more likely to be conformist, there is 'not a rigid bipolar model'. Some in lower streams conform and some in the academic streams become dissonant.

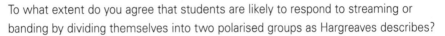

Task 5.2

To what extent do you agree that students are likely to respond to streaming or banding by dividing themselves into two polarised groups as Hargreaves describes?

Guidance
- Compare the findings of Woods on pupil adaptations.
- Now read the study by Stephen Ball (below) to find out if the lowest band necessarily has the worst behaviour.

Stephen Ball: banding and mixed-ability teaching

Stephen Ball conducted 3 years of detailed observations, interviews and an examination of secondary data at 'Beachside Comprehensive' (1981) to analyse how school processes, such as banding and teaching mixed ability groups, affected students' progress.

Students already in the second year at the beginning of his study had been divided into three broad-ability bands when they first entered the school. This had been carried out entirely on the basis of information from the primary feeder schools — Beachside did not conduct entry tests. Three of the four primary schools had submitted test scores in some subjects for some students, but these data were patchy. Ball concluded that reports by primary teachers strongly influenced the banding of students. He found a high correlation between the occupations of the students' parents and the bands they were placed in. About two-thirds of Band 1 students had parents in non-manual occupations compared with one-sixth of students in Band 2. He concluded that feeder schools' test scores did not fully determine the bands students were placed in; the primary teachers' impression of the students, based on their social backgrounds, had a significant effect.

Comprehensive schools were introduced to provide students from all social backgrounds with equal opportunity to succeed, as opposed to the selective system in which middle-class children were more likely to win places at grammar school. However, the processes of banding or streaming in comprehensive schools create similar divisions to the selective system, only within the one institution. If differentiation is based on subjective impressions rather than objective test scores it might be even more socially divisive.

Stephen Ball

> Pupils in many schools are still selected as they enter, or soon after, on much the same lines as they had been selected under the tripartite system; they go into the A-stream instead of to a grammar school or into the D-stream instead of to a secondary modern.
>
> S. Ball, *Beachside Comprehensive* (1981)

Band allocation at Beachside was, to some extent, a matter of chance; if too many students were initially considered for Band 1, further information was sought from the primary schools so some could be demoted. Yet once established in these bands, students were rarely moved. Students in Band 1 were taught at a faster pace, so it would have been difficult for a wrongly placed Band 2 student to move and catch up with the work missed. Band 3 students, the lowest ability group, were not a major disciplinary problem — many had acknowledged special needs and were treated accordingly. However, as soon as 'fine streaming' by subjects was replaced by the banding system, Band 2 classes became a major source of disruption. Once placed in Band 2, the misbehaviour in the class and the teaching styles and curriculum adopted made underachievement almost inevitable.

Ball used objective measures such as detention records to establish that discipline was indeed a problem in Band 2 classes. He also used the Flanders

interaction-analysis grid to monitor communication within lessons, finding far more examples of teachers rebuking students and justifying their authority in Band 2 lessons than in Band 1. He described a typical Band 2 biology lesson in which the teacher kept a constant eye open for disruptive behaviour, leaving less time to focus on the subject.

> As he pauses at each bench to check the pupils' work he looks round the room to check that all is well. At frequent intervals during his talk with the pupils his head pops up and down like a gopher from a hole, to recheck the class.
>
> *Teacher*: 'Wally, get on.'
>
> He looks down, up again.
>
> *Teacher*: 'Jim, your own book. Belinda, you too.'
>
> Down again and up.
>
> *Teacher*: 'Come on, you three, on your own please.'
>
> Down again and up, and down and up again.
>
> *Teacher*: 'Put that scarf away, Nigel, do I have to separate you three?'
>
> He stares at them for a second or two.
>
> *Teacher*: 'Are you eating, Max?'
>
> S. Ball, *Beachside Comprehensive* (1981)

In contrast, Band 1 lessons were orderly, teacher talk was almost exclusively about the subject, students were more often engaged in discussion than in simple copying tasks and more topics were covered. Also, Band 1 students studied more foreign languages. Thus, Band 1 students were much better prepared for examinations and professional careers.

Ball relates the banding in Beachside Comprehensive to labelling theory.

> As the band allocation of the pupils was a 'given', a label imposed from outside prior to any contact with the pupils, the teachers were 'taking', and deriving assumptions on the basis of, that label, rather than 'making' their own evaluation of the relative abilities of individual pupils.

The school timetable — where a teacher might have certain classes of over 30 students as infrequently as once or twice a week — meant that the teacher had little chance of getting to know all of the pupils well. This resulted in pupils being likely to be stereotyped according to their band. Contradictory information concerning a student's real potential may have been overlooked, which was particularly unfortunate for borderline students who might easily have been placed in a higher band. Some students would have performed poorly regardless of the banding system, yet many might not have.

> The estimated potential of the 2TA (Band 2) pupils based on the reports from their junior schools, which led to their being allocated to Band 2, was such as to label them 'failures' in a system that had not given them the opportunity to show their worth

(despite the rhetoric of equality of opportunity). This system required them to respect it and accept from it values which stressed the importance of hard work, enthusiasm, good behaviour and academic striving — even though, by assigning them to Band 2, the system had assumed and accepted that they would be lacking in these qualities.

Ball's interviews with teachers revealed that when the current second-year Band 2 students first started at Beachside they were enthusiastic about their work. However, by the second term, they had begun to conform to the stereotypes that staff applied to them and emerged as 'problem' pupils. Examination of registers showed an increasing gap in attendance patterns between Bands 1 and 2; fewer Band 2 students attended extra-curricular activities and by the second year, anti-school subcultures were clearly established. Band 2 students were responding to a lack of status within the school by rejecting its values.

Ball concluded his study by examining the school's first attempts to introduce mixed-ability teaching among younger students, but decided it was too early to assess its results. Nevertheless, he suggested that, in a competitive educational system, mixed-ability teaching is no guarantee of equal opportunities for children from all social backgrounds. The teacher in a mixed-ability class may still have preconceptions of different 'types' of children and rank them according to perceived academic ability. They are likely to be set different tasks and may receive varying amounts of encouragement, affecting their self-image and ambition. Eventually, they will be directed into different subject choices and examinations.

Ball concludes that comprehensive schools, even with mixed-ability teaching, a national curriculum and a common examination system such as GCSEs, will continue to be divisive as long as most teachers continue to think in terms of 'types' of children.

Task 5.3

Discuss the following questions:
(a) How practical is it to avoid streaming by ability, as Hargreaves recommended?
(b) Would mixed ability teaching reduce problems of underachievement by working-class students?
(c) There is evidence that streaming and setting have increased in secondary schools since the national curriculum was introduced. Why do you think this is, and what effect might it have on behaviour? Will it raise standards as hoped?

Guidance
(a) Draw on your own experience here.
(b) What does Stephen Ball say on this issue?
(c) If necessary, return to this question after reading Chapter 6.

How influential are pupil subcultures?

Some processes within schools — such as streaming and banding — might encourage the formation of anti-school subcultures because students feel rejected by the selection process. However, there is evidence that some groups of students have low expectations even before this happens.

In 1978, Angela McRobbie found girls in their early teens already planning a future geared around courtship and early marriage. Sue Sharpe's study of working-class girls in the same decade found similarly limited horizons, though when she replicated her study in 1994, girls of similar background expressed greater ambitions. In *Failing Working-Class Girls* (2000), Plummer notes:

> Working-class areas often lack any effective grapevine culture or general awareness about the possibilities of higher education for children or adults. Few people have any contact with anyone who has attended higher education, so they do not know how the system works and do not see its benefits.
>
> G. Plummer, Failing Working-Class Girls (2000)

Paul Willis's study of the subculture of working-class boys who saw no point in making efforts at school has already been mentioned. The 12 'lads' Willis studied closely modelled themselves on their fathers and other members of the working-class community that surrounded their secondary modern school. One of the boys, Spanksy, described his father thus:

> I'd like to be like him, you know, he can't stand no bull, if anyone tries it on him, he hates it…I'd love to be like him, he's a great bloke.
>
> Quoted in P. Willis, Learning to Labour: How Working Class Kids
Get Working Class Jobs (1978)

Willis's interviews with some of the boys' parents revealed a lack of respect for the values of the school. Spanksy's father was suspicious of the teachers' intentions on open night and described the head master as irritating and 'full of bull'.

Will's mother had told her son that she was keeping all the letters from the school about his drinking exploits and similar misbehaviour. The boy later recounted the incident to Willis:

> I says, 'What you keeping them for?' She says, 'Well, it'll be nice to look back on to, won't it, you know, show your kids like, you know, what a terror you was. I'm keeping 'em, I am'.
>
> Quoted in P. Willis, Learning to Labour: How Working Class Kids
Get Working Class Jobs (1978)

Willis argues that the shop-floor culture experienced by the boys' fathers involved 'a form of masculine chauvinism' and 'a massive attempt to gain informal control of the work process'. Men prided themselves on their physical toughness and their ability to outwit the management. Far from being down-trodden workers, they enjoyed playing practical jokes on each other, displayed sexist pin-ups and cared little for paper qualifications.

Willis argues that as students became disillusioned by school, forming a counter-culture with similar values to the shop floor enhanced their self-confidence but made academic failure almost inevitable. Unlike Hargreaves, he suggests the formation of such subcultures is not necessarily the result of grouping by supposed ability.

> It was by no means only the least able who were involved in the counter-school group. Some of its really central members were highly articulate, clear-sighted, assertive and able across a range of activities. They had decided that, for them and at that stage, the life of 'the lads' offered more than the conventional road…And those verging towards the anti-school perspective were, if anything, aided by the new forms of mixed-ability groupings, topic-centred teaching, student-centred teaching and the obvious confusion caused by the high number of group changes during the day.
>
> P. Willis, *Learning to Labour: How Working Class Kids Get Working Class Jobs* (1978)

Paul Willis's study shows that even well-meaning attempts at mixed-ability grouping and progressive teaching methods could do little to offset the influence of the students' social background and prior expectations, and that setting and teacher stereotyping make matters worse. Likewise, studies of ethnic minorities (examined earlier) show that prior experiences of racism can lead students to form defensive subcultures. Teachers may then stereotype them as potential troublemakers, controlling them more harshly than other students and sometimes interpreting their resulting alienation as grounds for assigning them to low-ability groups.

Task 5.4

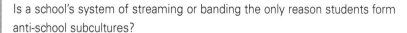

Is a school's system of streaming or banding the only reason students form anti-school subcultures?

Guidance

Consider:

- evidence from Willis
- Plummer's description of the working-class subculture she grew up in
- Mac an Ghaill's references to groups such as the Rastaheads and the Posse

John Abraham: divide and school

John Abraham's 1995 study shows that streaming, labelling and the formation of subcultures are interconnected and continue to affect school progress. He studied the effects of social class in a mixed comprehensive school through a detailed ethnographic study, interviewing students and teachers, using classroom observation and questionnaires and analysing school records.

To avoiding falling into the trap of banding pupils according to teacher impression, which Ball noted often follows social-class lines, 'Greenfield School' opted instead to set children according to their ability in each subject from Year 8. Despite best intentions, students were nearly always put in sets of a similar level for every subject. The sets closely reflected their social-class origins, based on parental occupation.

Abraham found that teachers made judgements about the likely behaviour of sets of pupils before meeting them. One said:

> When you get your next year's timetable and you can see that it's a top or bottom set then you get certain images. If you get a top set you tend to think that their behaviour will be better. You tend to think with a bottom set you will get more discipline problems.
>
> Quoted in J. Abraham, *Divide and School: Gender and Class Dynamics in Comprehensive Education* (1995)

He found this led teachers to respond differently to classroom deviance. He described a student in a top set being merely reprimanded for inattention, whereas behaviour not much worse in a lower set resulted in the culprit being sent to the work centre — a sort of 'sin bin' for badly behaved students. He observed this punishment being used frequently for lower-set and middle-set students but never for top sets and he believed that it increased students' rejection of school values and increased their desire to leave. Through differentiated punishments, teachers 'unconsciously discriminate against working-class pupils because they are mainly to be found in the lower sets'.

The school had a formal system of bad-behaviour notes and missed-assignment reports, which were kept in students' records. By analysing these, Abraham was able to compare the students' behaviour when they were in year 7 mixed-ability groups with their behaviour after setting in year 8. Students who eventually ended up in top and bottom sets had similar numbers of notes during year 7, but in year 8 those in lower sets had far more. Abraham interpreted this as evidence that differentiation by the school led to polarisation in student behaviour. Those who felt labelled as having less academic potential reacted by developing anti-school attitudes, which then further undermined their chances of success.

Task 5.5

Look again at Abraham's analysis of bad-behaviour notes. Are there other possible explanations for the data besides the one he suggested?

Guidance

Consider the content of the paragraph preceding the one about bad-behaviour notes.

Abraham also studied polarisation in friendship choices. He asked Year-10 students to list their six closest friends and any students they particularly did not get on with. They tended to choose friends who were similarly ranked in the setting system. Follow-up interviews showed that former friends in different sets were dropped less because of infrequent contact than because of different attitudes to school.

Student: Last year I used to have a friend Charley (Charley was in the top sets for English, mathematics and French) but this year he doesn't speak to me any more and every time I see him he's hanging around with boffins like.

JA: What are boffins?

Student: People who work. Stay in all the time. Never go out, go down the town or nothing. And always get good letters home and pats on the back by teachers.

Quoted in J. Abraham, *Divide and School* (1995)

Interviews with top-stream students conveyed desire for academic progress and preference for strict teachers, who could help them achieve. They had a pro-school value system, whereas those in lower sets typically liked teachers who were more lax. One such student told Abraham:

You can have a laugh because he can't control the class so you can take advantage.

This preference influenced their subject options. Those in lower sets sometimes chose subjects where the teacher was known not to be able to control the class and avoided those where teachers punished students for not doing their homework.

As might be expected, students in lower sets tended to choose more practical options in line with the manual occupations of their parents; students in higher sets generally chose more academic subjects and aspired to professional careers. Interviews with students about how much parental advice they received in these choices revealed that middle-class parents involved themselves far more in the process, frequently directing their children towards more academic choices. Apart from parents discouraging girls from choosing 'masculine' subjects, working-class pupils were usually left to decide for themselves. Middle-set pupils, whose parents were often manual workers, tended to aspire to

non-manual careers — the only evidence against a simple reproduction of social-class patterns.

Abraham concludes:

> Streaming by sets is likely to accentuate social class differences in academic performance at school. Evidently, streaming by sets is inconsistent with the egalitarian and integrative comprehensive ideals of bringing pupils together from different social class backgrounds with a view to reducing social class inequalities and increasing social solidarity.
>
> Quoted in J. Abraham, *Divide and School* (1995)

Other school factors

Different quality schools

Michael Rutter's research in 1979, entitled *Fifteen Thousand Hours: Secondary Schools and their Effects on Children*, changed the focus away from small-group interaction to the differences between schools. He found that students from similar social backgrounds had different achievement levels depending on which of 12 inner-London secondary schools they attended. Though class differences in attainment remained, higher results were obtained in schools that were well organised, with emphasis on academic achievement, in which teachers were punctual and well prepared for lessons, and where there was more emphasis on reward than punishment. Many of these points would be likely to encourage positive self-concepts in the students.

Since 1988, differences between schools have been highlighted by the publication of league tables. The possible effect on student progress is the subject of Chapter 6.

The hidden curriculum

A factor likely to operate in all schools is the hidden curriculum. Marxists note how the regimentation of under 16s, especially in lower-ability groups in state schools, prepares them for working lives as underlings. Post-16 students destined for professional careers are trusted more and given privileges, such as the use of a common room.

The hidden curriculum contains messages about ethnicity and gender. Asian languages are rarely studied in mainstream schools and there are few references to non-Western or female scientists, artists and musicians. History ('his story') is mainly about the deeds of men. Teachers may exaggerate gender differences by organising boys against girls in competitions, asking boys to perform heavy jobs and girls to prepare refreshments.

High culture is a more significant part of the school curriculum than popular culture, making middle-class children feel more at ease with what is being taught and the language in which it is expressed.

Which school factor is most important?

Many factors within schools affect how well students perform. However, it is difficult to separate the effects of ability grouping, teacher expectation and pupil subculture, as they are closely interrelated. In addition, some students receive more of the sort of knowledge that examiners value at schools that are better run. Thus, despite frequent government attempts to reform the education system and raise standards, inequalities continue.

Summary

- Interactionists have identified processes within schools that affect attainment.
- According to labelling studies, teachers assume students will be either more or less academically successful, basing their judgements on social characteristics and appearance.
- Stereotyping students results in differentiated treatment, which can lead to a self-fulfilling prophecy.
- Studies of streaming and banding show that selection often reflects social origin.
- Students in 'lower-ability' groups often respond to teachers' lower expectations by underperforming.
- Anti-school subcultures often arise in lower bands, resulting in disruption and poor attainment.
- Mixed-ability teaching still entails differentiating between students because of the demands of examination courses. Education is competitive.
- Streaming, labelling and the formation of subcultures are interconnected and continue to affect school progress.
- Schools differ in quality, producing different results with similar types of student.
- The hidden curriculum, with its messages about ethnicity, gender and class, may disadvantage some groups.

Task 5.6

Examine the role of processes within schools in producing different educational achievement among pupils from different social groups. (20 marks)

Guidance

This essay question needs careful planning. Initially, select material from this chapter and make notes under the headings:

- labelling
- ability groups
- subcultures

You will need to explain that the formation of subcultures may sometimes occur outside school, but that school processes, such as teacher stereotyping and banding, are likely to consolidate existing subcultures and give rise to new ones.

In response to the phrase 'different social groups', look back at the chapters about ethnicity, class and gender, and select at least one named study to illustrate how processes within schools affect each group. Strictly speaking, the sexes are biological groups but emphasis on differences between them is social. If in an examination paper there were a separate question on gender, it would be wise to focus mainly on ethnicity and class in response to this question.

To gain evaluation marks, link and contrast the work of different researchers, pointing out, for example, how they disagree about whether mixed-ability teaching solves the problems of poor motivation. Comment briefly on the effectiveness of the research methods used.

In your conclusion, assess the importance of various factors or suggest how they interconnect.

Research suggestion

Conduct sensitive interviews or distribute carefully worded questionnaires asking students how they responded to being banded or streamed at various points in their school careers. Was their motivation affected? Did they notice behaviour patterns changing if they moved from a mixed-ability to a streamed situation? Were teacher attitudes and expectations different? Do students like to be divided by ability and, if so, why?

Useful websites

- History of Education account of Rosenthal and Jacobson's experiment
  http://fcis.oise.utoronto.ca/~daniel_sch/assignment1/1968rosenjacob.html

- Studies of teacher pupil relationships
  www.sociology.org.uk/tece1ez4.htm

Video

- HaloVine video: Paul Willis on *Learning to Labour*

Further reading

- Abraham, J. (1995) *Divide and School: Gender and Class Dynamics in Comprehensive Education*, Falmer Press.
- Ball, S. (ed.) (2004) *The RoutledgeFalmer Reader in Sociology of Education*, RoutledgeFalmer.
- Hargreaves, A. and Woods, P. (eds) (1984) *Classrooms and Staffrooms: Sociology of Teachers and Teaching*, Open University Press.

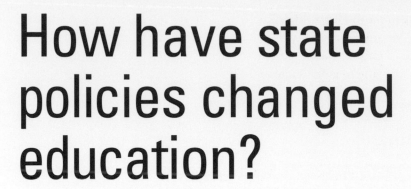

How have state policies changed education?

Few days go by without some reference in the news to government plans for education. Tony Blair is famous for commenting in 1997 that 'education, education, education' were his three priorities, but the subject has been of central concern to governments since at least the mid-nineteenth century.

Just as sociologists disagree about the purposes of education, politicians have debated how different types of children should be educated, what schools should be like, the extent to which education needs to relate to employment and how standards can be improved.

Why was schooling made compulsory?

Before 1870, education in Britain was only available to the prosperous — who paid to attend public and grammar schools — and to a minority of the poor through charity, church and dame schools.

The 1870 Education Act encouraged school boards to build new non-denominational elementary schools, charging no more than nine pence a week. Most of the poor attended and by 1880 education became compulsory up to at least age ten. The aim was to teach the literacy and numeracy needed to put British industry on a par with foreign competitors. The poor should not be encouraged to entertain ideas above their station in life, but it was hoped that they would read their Bibles and be less easily swayed to revolution than ignorant peasants. Learning was basic, conducted in large numbers and often by rote, with a strong emphasis on obedience.

The number of grammar schools was increased under the 1902 Act. These, like the public schools, offered a wider curriculum and prepared people for the professions. Whether students attended these or the elementary schools was determined by income, not ability. Although the leaving age was extended to 14 by 1918, most pupils spent the whole of their education in elementary schools, which became free of charge in 1891.

Was the selective education system fair?

After the Second World War, there was a desire to create a fairer society, so free, state-run secondary education became available for all. The old elementary schools became primary schools and most children changed schools at 11. It was thought that different types of children would benefit from secondary education in three kinds of school, known together as the tripartite system:

- Grammar schools offered academic subjects and examinations to those able to pass intelligence tests — the '11 plus'. Only about 20% 'passed'.
- Technical and commercial schools were available for those with practical aptitude. Very few were built, taking only 5% of pupils.
- Secondary modern schools offered a less academic curriculum, with few examinations, until project-based CSEs began in the 1960s.

Weaknesses of the selective system

By the 1960s, opposition had built up to the tripartite system. The reasons for this were as follows:

- Although the schools were supposed to have 'parity of esteem' with equally good facilities and staff, inevitably, passing the 11-plus carried more prestige than failing it, so parents and well-qualified teachers generally preferred grammar schools.
- Students' self-esteem was lowered when they failed the exam, which could lead to underachievement.
- Intelligence tests might be inaccurate indicators of potential. Cultural capital, motivation and the amount of practice received are factors that could affect results.
- Late developers or incorrectly placed students found it difficult to transfer from secondary modern to grammar schools because the schools taught different subjects.
- A higher pass mark was required of girls than of boys because boys were thought to be later developers. Some girls who outperformed boys at 11 were rejected in order to keep the ratio of the sexes balanced in grammar schools.

- Some areas had fewer grammar school places or a higher than average proportion of able pupils, some of whom had to be refused places.
- Social democrats (moderate left wingers) such as A. H. Halsey argued that children already educationally disadvantaged by working-class backgrounds were less likely to pass the 11-plus. They went to secondary modern schools, whereas middle-class children tended to go to grammar schools.
- The few working-class children who were selected for grammar schools often felt uncomfortable there and many dropped out early.
- Lack of social mobility for most of the working class was a waste of individual potential and their inferior education made the British workforce less effective than global competitors.
- In the early years of the secondary moderns, students left school with no academic qualifications. This was about three-quarters of the population!

How satisfactory is the comprehensive system?

The Labour Party proposed comprehensive schools as a fairer alternative to the selective system. Children of all abilities would be taught in the same local school so that all had access to the same facilities and a wide curriculum. There would be no entrance exams to label the majority as failures and mixing of social classes would produce a less divided society. Ideas had changed about the nature of intelligence. While in the 1940s psychologists such as Cyril Burt had viewed it as largely inherited and fixed, the current view that a good education can stimulate students' intelligence became influential.

Conservatives generally opposed the comprehensive ideal, still advocating separate education for different abilities and fearing that the more able would be held back. This is close to the functionalist view that society needs leaders and that in a meritocracy those with ability should be promoted to fit such roles. Old Labour's view was closer to the Marxist one — that the children of the proletariat were being held back by the dominant bourgeoisie.

In 1965, the Labour Government asked local education authorities to reorganise their secondary schools as comprehensives. Most did, but the action was halted after the Conservatives were elected in 1970, resulting in the continued existence of a few grammar schools. By 1997, when New Labour gained power, they were more concerned about raising standards and providing parental choice than they were about closing the remaining grammar schools. Though they allowed parental ballots to shut down unsuccessful grammar schools, there are still over 160 grammar schools in existence, which seem unlikely to close in the near future.

Weaknesses and strengths of the comprehensive system

Weaknesses

- Independent schools, and the grammar schools that remain in some areas, attract many of the more able pupils away from local comprehensives. A school is not truly comprehensive if top-ability students have been 'creamed off' in this way — it is more like a secondary modern.
- Many comprehensives draw predominantly from a locality housing one social group, so the ideal of students mixing with those of different backgrounds may not be realised.
- Most comprehensive schools operate streaming or banding. Pupils in lower-ability streams may suffer from low self-esteem, similar to '11-plus failures'. Able children may be bullied.
- Research suggests that streaming is sometimes based on teacher labelling relating to class and ethnic background rather than on test results. Where there is a mixed catchment area, top streams tend to be dominated by the middle class, while lower streams consist mainly of working-class students.
- Many comprehensives are very large, creating problems of anonymity and control.
- Some comprehensives have been allowed to select a proportion of students either by general ability or, in the case of specialist schools, by specific aptitude. Though the government discourages it, oversubscribed schools may interview students with their parents and choose those from the most promising backgrounds.
- Comprehensives vary greatly in reputation. Affluent families desert 'bog-standard comprehensives', if necessary, moving house to increase their children's chance of being accepted by a more prestigious comprehensive. Working-class parents have less choice.

Strengths

- Comprehensives better satisfy social democrat demands for equal opportunities. Children of all income groups attend comprehensives, so there is more potential for social mobility.
- Students entering comprehensives are likely to feel more positive than those sent to secondary modern schools after failing the 11-plus. (Evidence

suggests that students assigned to low bands in comprehensive schools lose motivation later because the 'labelling' is less obvious).

- Tutor groups are often organised along mixed-ability lines, even when teaching groups are not. This promotes some social mixing.
- It is easier for a late developer to move into a higher band, or a higher set for a particular subject, than to move schools.
- Research has suggested that students of high ability do as well in comprehensives as in grammar schools and that lower-ability students achieve more than in secondary moderns.
- Comprehensive schools usually provide a wide range of examination options, including academic and vocational subjects at various levels.
- Being larger than the grammar and secondary modern schools that preceded them, comprehensive schools are more likely to have extensive facilities for sport, drama, technology and science.

Task 6.1

Identify *two* reasons why some parents are better able than others to choose which school their child attends.

Guidance

- Select some of the weaknesses and strengths of the comprehensive system from the list above.
- Consider the independent sector and the cost of fares to send a child to a distant school.

What is meant by progressive education?

By the 1960s, education, particularly in primary schools, had changed dramatically from the dry memorisation of facts favoured in the first elementary schools. Influenced by the work of child psychologists such as Jean Piaget, liberals such as Dewey and the general atmosphere of freedom pervasive in the second half of the 'swinging sixties', teacher-centred 'chalk-and-talk' methods had been replaced by child-centred education through exploration. This often entailed open-plan classrooms where children pursued different chosen activities at the same time.

Children engaged in a variety of activities in a 'progressive' open-plan setting

In secondary schools, there was more group work and project work, and students were encouraged to question traditional viewpoints. Learning to think was emphasised above knowing particular facts. This was known as progressive education.

Opposition to progressive education

In 1975–76 there was a public enquiry into the running of the William Tyndale primary school in north London, where some radical teachers were accused of encouraging revolution, teaching the children how to make crossbows instead of focusing on literacy and numeracy. Such children would be unemployable.

This case led politicians, especially the Conservative opposition, to conclude that British students lacked the skills of foreign competitors because of progressive education. Teachers had been allowed to teach more or less what they liked, except to examination classes. There had been too little time devoted to correctness in basic skills and too much time having noisy fun, being creative and learning subversive ideas from left-wing teachers.

It was necessary to ensure that schools prepared children better for the workplace. Academic standards could be raised by prescribing the essentials of a curriculum and testing to ensure that it was followed. The influence on schools of individual teachers, and, according to the Conservatives, Labour LEAs needed to be controlled. These initiatives subsequently led to the 'new vocationalism' under Labour and the Education Reform Act of 1988, under the Conservatives.

Vocational initiatives

In a high-profile speech in 1976, the Prime Minister, James Callaghan, said that there was a need to educate appropriately skilled and motivated young workers. It was a time of high unemployment, especially among school leavers, and in the great debate that followed many expressed the view that Britain would be more competitive if students received vocational (work-related) preparation in schools.

The Technical and Vocational Educational Initiative

In 1983, the Technical and Vocational Educational Initiative (TVEI) was set up to promote vocational awareness in secondary schools. Funding was provided for staff to organise work experience during school time and, alongside the normal curriculum for 14–18-year-olds, more computing and technology were encouraged.

National Vocational Qualifications

From 1986, National Vocational Qualifications (NVQs) were introduced for those over-16s who preferred employer-based training to school courses. Specific industries were to decide which skills were vocationally relevant and award certificates at various levels to those who acquired them. Theoretically, suitably qualified youth would then easily find work in the same field. However, in practice, employers still preferred school-leavers with academic qualifications. The Smithers Report revealed that the skills taught were often elementary and that there was pressure for everyone to pass, so the qualifications were worth little.

School-based vocational qualifications

General National Vocational Qualifications were introduced in 1992 to provide training at various levels in broad areas of work such as Health and Social Care, Business Studies, Applied ICT and Leisure and Tourism. Despite the government's promotion of these courses, the public continued to view vocational courses as less prestigious than academic ones and able students steered away from them. To improve their image, Blair's government renamed them Applied GCSEs and A-levels. These courses are more project-based than most GCSEs and A-levels and are available at some schools and most colleges of further education. An Applied GCSE or A-level counts as a double award and can be studied alongside traditional academic subjects.

Youth training

A major initiative to reduce the number of unemployed school-leavers was developed in the 1980s. Instead of receiving welfare benefits, 16 and 17-year-old unemployed people received a grant to work for an employer, who in exchange for a government subsidy, had to provide training. Unfortunately, there was less centralised supervision than in apprenticeship schemes in other countries such as Germany. While some employers provided high-quality training and offered the young good careers afterwards, others used them as cheap labour and taught them little. The popularity of the scheme quickly diminished and most young people capable of doing so found work, stayed on at school or attended college.

Critics, such as Dan Finn, claim that the Youth Training Scheme (YTS) was set up for the wrong reasons:

- High youth unemployment occurred because there were not enough jobs. The problem lay in the economy, not in young people's lack of skills. Job creation was needed instead.
- The scheme was introduced to improve the government's image — those young people on YTS did not appear in the unemployment figures.
- Young people were accused of being work-shy. YTS was intended to teach them better work habits such as punctuality. This was victim blaming. In truth, young people were prepared to work when jobs were available; many students squeezed part-time work into their busy lives.

They also say that general vocational training is less useful than learning specific skills in a real job when the time comes.

In 1997, New Labour adapted YTS into a scheme called the New Deal. This 'welfare-to-work' scheme was designed as part of the 'stakeholder economy' — everyone has a stake in society and has responsibilities for it. The placements offering work experience were extended to include the voluntary sector and environment taskforces. The scheme involved day release for education or training, leading to a qualification. By 2000, 345,000 young people in the New Deal scheme had found work. However, this might have happened anyway as the economy had improved.

Should education be organised with only work in mind?

- Universal education began in elementary schools with a limited curriculum aimed at producing a literate workforce.

- Secondary modern schools had a narrow vocational emphasis.
- Attitudes gradually changed, putting more emphasis on equality of opportunity and, during the 1960s and 1970s, on enjoyment of learning for its own sake.
- The new comprehensive schools offered a broad curriculum, including such courses as social studies and design for living, alongside traditional subjects.
- However, by 1994, a government White Paper was recommending that after the age of 14, some students could concentrate on vocational courses such as Part 1 GNVQs. Opponents felt that the working-class students channelled into such courses would be disadvantaged in a similar way to students in secondary modern schools. Traditional academic qualifications are still the best route to good jobs.

Box 6.1

The new tripartite system?

Critics suggest that with new vocationalism, a new tripartite system has emerged:

- Middle-class students continue to take traditional A-levels, followed by university and training for a profession. As they realise that there are few unskilled jobs for 16-year-olds and that employers prefer academic qualifications, more people are opting for this route.
- Vocational school and college courses tend to attract the less able, so the job prospects at the end are less promising.
- The numbers in youth training have declined to those who have few other options. When they are too old for the scheme, many take dead-end jobs or become unemployed.

Why was education reformed in 1988?

In response to fears that British youth lacked the skills needed to be efficient workers competing in world markets, other initiatives besides vocational ones were taken to improve the education system. Many of these were included in the 1988 Education Reform Act.

The Act included the following terms:

- **National curriculum** This was established for pupils from 5 to 16 years in state schools. The core subjects of English, mathematics and science were to occupy 30–40% of teaching time. Seven foundation subjects, including technology and a foreign language (in secondary schools), were to be taught. For practical reasons, the list has since been slimmed down.

- **National standardised attainment tests (SATs)** Tests in English, mathematics and science at the ages of 7, 11, 14 and 16 were introduced to check if the attainment targets had been reached by students. These results were to be published in league tables to encourage schools' effectiveness. (Baseline tests at 5 years have since been introduced to measure 'value added'.)
- **Open enrolment** Parents could send their children to any non-selective school that had places. This would encourage schools to perform better than in the past, when children had to attend their catchment-area school.
- **Formula funding** Schools received funds according to how many students they attracted. Failing schools would close through lack of resources and successful schools could afford to expand.
- **Local management of schools** This meant school heads and governors had more say over control of their finances, restricting the influence of local education authorities.
- **City technology colleges** These were partly sponsored by industry. They brought more IT and links with business into their curricula, underlining the importance of vocational education. Other schools were encouraged to become grant-maintained, opting out of LEA control and receiving funding directly from the government (though this was eventually phased out).

Inspections by OFSTED every 4 years would ensure that these recommendations were followed.

Criticisms of the Education Reform Act

The Act ensured that subjects considered essential were made available to every state-school student. Subjects were subdivided into topics and skills to be taught at particular key stages, so that students moving schools could adapt fairly easily and teachers could assume what should already have been covered by new classes. Basic skills were less likely to be neglected in schools. However, problems arose:
- Keeping records of the progress of each individual student at each key stage takes time away from classroom teaching and lesson preparation. Teachers' protests brought some initial improvements. However, recent government initiatives concerning pupil data, target setting and tracking have once again increased administrative workloads.
- Test results could lead to children being labelled as having more, or less, potential from an early age — a divisive step.
- In their eagerness to score well in league tables, schools might try to select more able students, which is contrary to the comprehensive principle.
- Gillborn and Youdell (2000) found that schools were giving more help to students who were likely, but not certain, to gain five or more GCSEs at grade

C or above, which is the statistic published in league tables. Students confident of achieving this level, and those with little hope of doing so, received less attention. Certain groups, such as special needs students and some ethnic minorities, were likely to be neglected as a consequence.

- The progress schools make with disadvantaged pupils is not acknowledged in league tables, which compare comprehensive schools with selective schools. Early league tables gave raw scores, with no indication of the social circumstances of schools. Recent attempts to indicate special needs and 'value added' still provide an incomplete picture.

- Despite open enrolment, some parents have more choice than others. More prosperous parents can afford to transport their children some distance from home to an acclaimed school and may have the influence to get them admitted. Poorer and ethnic-minority parents may have to accept an inferior local school.

- An LEA is less able to achieve balanced planning if many schools in the area opt out of its control.

- Education has become marketised. Stephen Ball suggests that the measures above have combined to create a materialistic, competitive atmosphere in which commercial, rather than educational, principles are increasingly dominant. This reflects the free-enterprise values of the Conservatives who produced the Act, but does little to meet the needs of disadvantaged pupils. Some schools have become more like businesses. They use funds that should be spent on education to employ marketing staff who promote the schools through glossy brochures and press coverage. Mac an Ghaill's criticisms of the new enterprise culture in Parnell School are discussed in Chapter 3.

Task 6.2

Identify and briefly describe two reasons why a school's position in examination 'league tables' may be an unsatisfactory measure of its worth or effectiveness. (8 marks)

Guidance
- Choose two very different points, answering each in a separate paragraph. You could provide an example of a specific problem a school might need to overcome that would not be shown in league tables. You could also suggest a non-academic achievement that would not appear in tables.
- Use a key phrase for each idea and then explain in two or three sentences why the data may disguise the school's real achievements.

Introduction of GCSEs

Since the comprehensive reorganisation, increasing equality of opportunity has been less of a government priority. Preparing students for work and raising standards in basic skills have become the major focus. However, the introduction of GCSE examinations in 1988 was an exception.

GCSEs replaced a two-tier system of O-levels for academic students and easier, coursework-based CSEs for the rest. This was felt to be divisive, especially as candidates were usually separated into appropriate streams 2 years in advance. The new exams catered for most levels of ability, incorporated coursework and gave credit for what students knew, rather than penalising gaps in their knowledge.

Although teachers and students generally welcomed the new courses, they were soon modified because the government felt that a high proportion of coursework marked by teachers meant that standards between schools could not be compared easily. In line with the general aims of the 1988 Act, the coursework component of GCSEs has been drastically cut, specifications in subjects such as English have become more prescriptive and there are penalties in examinations for poor basic skills.

Educational changes, post-16
Curriculum 2000

In 1996, the Conservative Party Review of Qualifications for 16–19-year-olds recommended preserving the 'gold standard' of A-levels while giving greater status to vocational courses. As in the International Baccalaureate, students would have to study a wide range of subjects to qualify for an Advanced Diploma.

After a change of government, many details were modified and the diploma was postponed. However, the AS/A2 system emerged:

- Four or five AS subjects should be studied in Year 12, to increase *breadth* of knowledge and encourage more students to continue with mathematics, sciences and languages.
- In Year 13, most students would continue three subjects at A2, to achieve *depth* of knowledge and A-level standard.
- Key skills qualifications in communication, IT and application of numbers would ensure that students continued to develop the basic skills valued by employers.

A problem with the AS year has been work overload for students. This has caused many schools to drop key skills, though some have recently taken up critical thinking instead. The system was intended to ensure that all students studied science, mathematics, a foreign language and arts, humanities or social sciences up to the age of 18. However, the existing four subjects at AS and three at A2 structure scarcely broadens students' knowledge.

The Tomlinson Report, 2004

A more radical attempt to overhaul 14–19 education was outlined in the Tomlinson Report:

- GCSEs, A-levels and vocational qualifications would be replaced by a diploma accessible at four levels. This could reduce the number of examinations students currently sit.
- The diploma would have a compulsory core, maintaining the priority of the key skills of literacy, numeracy and IT.
- Coursework units in particular subjects would be replaced by a single extended project of the student's choice.

Andy Davey (*Guardian*, 24 February 2005)

- Students would specialise in academic or vocational subjects or a combination. Those who chose a vocational pathway would spend some time with training providers, reducing the alienation of less academic students and increasing their chances of obtaining good employment.
- In the examinations equivalent to A-level, there would be some extra, highly demanding questions, enabling the most gifted students to be identified, unlike the situation with current grade As.
- Study skills, problem solving, community service, work experience, sport and creative activities would enrich the curriculum.

The intention was to implement the Tomlinson proposals over a decade. There has already been resistance to the abolition of GCSEs and A-levels. Current indications are that coursework may be removed from A-levels in 2008, in preparation for the extended project, but how far other aspects of the proposal will be fulfilled is, as yet, unclear.

Education maintenance allowances

Since 2004, students from low-income families following post-16 academic and vocational courses at school and further education colleges have received grants. Receiving these grants is dependent on good attendance and making progress. Their provision is to discourage students from dropping out of education in favour of paid work.

University changes

In 1993, in a further bid to encourage young people to seek higher qualifications, polytechnics were allowed to become universities and the number of student places for degree courses was increased, particularly in sciences. This was partially funded by gradually replacing student grants with loans to be paid back after the completion of the course.

Universities soon found that government funding was inadequate to meet the cost of educating the extra students, so tuition fees were introduced by the Higher Education Act of 1997. Increases to £3000 per year were permitted from 2006.

Though there are some concessions for students from very low-income families, the burden of having to repay large student loans may discourage some able young people from continuing in higher education. This is a reversal of the postwar drive to encourage working-class students into universities by giving them full grants. Universities have now developed into a two-tier system with ex-polytechnics at the bottom. The system could become even more divisive if more prestigious universities decide to charge higher-than-average fees.

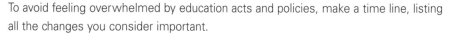

Task 6.3

To avoid feeling overwhelmed by education acts and policies, make a time line, listing all the changes you consider important.

Guidance
You could include colour coding to distinguish policies prioritising vocationalism, equal opportunities and raising standards.

Raising standards or tackling inequalities?

Since taking office in 1997, New Labour has introduced many educational initiatives. These aim to raise academic standards, increase parental choice and help the socially excluded, but some are controversial.

New Labour initiatives

Education action zones

From 1998, additional funding was given to disadvantaged areas to set up breakfast clubs, homework clubs, summer literacy and numeracy schemes, and to pay for master classes, special needs teaching, mentors or whatever local needs were identified. Some schemes are sponsored by industry. Like previous compensatory education schemes, such as education priority areas in Britain and Operation Head Start in the USA, education action zones cannot address the material problems of poorer children.

SureStart

This network of organisations was set up in 2000 'to work with parents-to-be, parents and children to provide for the physical, intellectual and social development of babies and young children — particularly those who are disadvantaged — so that they can flourish at home and when they get to school, and thereby break the cycle of disadvantage for the current generation of young children'.

Beacon and leading-edge schools

Successful schools receive additional funding to involve staff and students from local partner schools in beneficial activities and to 'share good practice', raising standards throughout. Schemes involving partner schools with large proportions of ethnic-minority or working-class children are most likely to be funded. Likewise, Excellence in Cities involves clusters of schools working together to organise stimulating activities for gifted students, who might otherwise be a neglected minority.

Specialist schools and city academies

Specialist schools receive extra funding for giving priority to a particular subject and involving other schools in projects relating to it.

City academies are publicly funded schools, to which private sponsors contribute financially in exchange for a say in the curriculum, ethos and staffing. They are encouraged to specialise, so they are allowed to select up to 10% of students with aptitude for the specialist subject. They have replaced 'failing' comprehensive schools in disadvantaged areas and have met with a mixed reception.

- Critics argue that because they are oversubscribed, city academies can 'cherry pick' more able students to boost their results, which reduces the academic quality of the intake at other local comprehensives.
- Supporters point to the large proportion of children on free school meals in the academies and the fact that local people feel a new sense of hope when an unsuccessful school has been closed and replaced.

Higher Standards, Better Schools for All

In 2005, the government White Paper *Higher Standards, Better Schools for All* proposed expansion of the new city academies, planning to open 200 in areas of previous school failure by 2010.

Other state primary and secondary comprehensive schools are to become trust or foundation schools, meaning that they will no longer be under direct local authority control. They will be able to choose to be more diverse, reflecting the requirements of local parents, for example by acquiring specialisms. Currently, some students have to travel long distances because there are insufficient appropriate school places in their locality. Under this new legislation, parents can organise a new neighbourhood trust school to meet their children's needs. Some will be extended schools, offering additional support after normal hours.

The White Paper is ambiguous about how students will be chosen for trust schools, saying that the schools can 'set their own admissions arrangements'. Though supporters of the White Paper deny that this would be on grounds of ability, opponents are suspicious that it might bring 'selection by the back door'.

Many left-wing MPs, including John Prescott, opposed the plans. Prescott claimed that there is a danger that the new city academies could become grammar schools by another name. A two-tier system could develop, of inferior comprehensive schools for the majority and superior city academies, operating their own admissions policies, for the children of ambitious, middle-class parents, who are sufficiently well informed to seek the best for their children.

It remains to be seen how the implementation of these proposals will affect equal opportunities and student progress. Different critics fear that either trust schools or city academies will select students, affecting the comprehensive intake of the alternatives. Tony Blair denies this. Unlike Prescott, he assumes that parents of all classes have sufficient interest in, and knowledge about, the rapidly changing school system to be able to insist on the best for their children.

John Prescott opposed Tony Blair's 2005 White Paper

Contrary to the evidence from Hargreaves and Ball, the White Paper recommends more setting by subject ability to raise standards. Blair believes that disadvantaged children will progress alongside others as less effective schools are forced to improve or be closed down by parents eager to set up better trust schools. This faith in the interest and wisdom of parents as consumers is in line with the notion of education as a marketplace that was introduced by the Conservatives in 1988 and which has since been developed by New Labour.

What are the main debates in the sociology of UK education?

The disagreement between Prescott and Blair reflects wider debates within education:

- To what extent should schools be controlled by central government, LEAs, local parents, businesses, religious groups or other independent bodies?
- Are there dangers in allowing those not working in education to influence the curriculum and ethos of a school?

- Should there be so many specialist schools and so much emphasis on vocational skills?
- Does competition between schools benefit all students, as supporters of marketisation claim?
- Does streaming by subject ability raise standards in all groups?
- To what extent can changes in the education system alone influence disadvantages relating to gender, ethnicity and social class?

Summary

- State-run elementary schooling became compulsory in 1880. The purpose was to teach children basic skills needed for employment.
- In 1944, the selective tripartite system provided secondary education for all.
- From 1965, the comprehensive system for children of all abilities gradually replaced the selective system. However, independent and grammar schools 'creamed off' some more able students and many inequalities remained.
- A backlash against progressive education in the mid-1970s led to the new vocationalism, emphasising the need to prepare students for work.
- In 1988, the Education Reform Act brought a national curriculum, rigorously tested by a government concerned with raising standards. Open enrolment, formula funding (see page 109) and the publication of league tables led to the marketisation of schools competing for students.
- Also in 1988, GCSEs were developed to cater for students of most abilities.
- In 2000, AS qualifications were introduced to broaden the post-16 curriculum, with the inclusion of key skills to develop attributes approved by employers. The Tomlinson Report recommended more dramatic 14–19 changes, proposing a diploma, with both vocational and academic pathways, to replace GCSEs and A-levels.
- Student finances have been affected by education maintenance allowances and the introduction of university tuition fees.
- Recent initiatives to raise standards have included education action zones, leading-edge schools, specialist schools and city academies.
- The 2005 White Paper has recommended further controversial changes, such as expanding city academies and encouraging other schools to become trust schools, with control over their own curriculum and admissions. Critics fear that, by selection, some of these schools may undermine the comprehensive system.

Chapter 6

Research suggestion

Investigate the schools in your area by searching for a list on the internet and then finding out what different types there are. Interview students and/or parents to discover reasons for their choice of school, whether it is the nearest and whether they really feel they benefit from choice.

Task 6.4

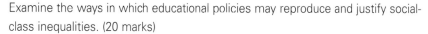

Examine the ways in which educational policies may reproduce and justify social-class inequalities. (20 marks)

Guidance

- 'Policies' include legislation, such as the 1944 Act, movements such as new vocationalism and progressive education and initiatives such as education action zones, Excellence in Cities and SureStart. Policies can also entail leaving a situation unchanged, such as allowing grammar and independent schools to co-exist alongside the comprehensive system. Anything recommended in a government White Paper, such as increasing streaming or extending school hours, is also a policy.
- Use the time-line suggested in Task 6.3 to identify which policies, since 1870, relate to social class. Decide which ones are the most significant, as there may be insufficient time to discuss them all.
- In describing each policy, preferably in chronological order, clarify its main aim and identify how different social classes were affected, *intentionally or not*. The tripartite system is a clear case of class reproduction. The 1988 Act, though its emphasis was on raising standards throughout, resulted in schools with working-class intakes losing formula funding (see page 109).
- Ensure that you explain the phrase 'reproduce and justify social-class inequalities' early on and use it, throughout the body of the essay and in the conclusion, to emphasise the relevance of your points.
- Give some thought to the conclusion. You may decide that any policy that offers vocational and academic routes or encourages parents to make choices may disadvantage the working class.

Useful websites

- 'City academies are achieving great results without deserting the poor', by Jacqui Smith
  http://education.guardian.co.uk/schools/comment/story/0,9828,1642785,00.html

- Higher Standards: Better Schools for All, White Paper on Education 2005
  www.dfes.gov.uk/publications/schoolswhitepaper/pdfs/
  DfES-Schools%20White%20 Paper.pdf

Further reading

- Ball, S. (2003) *Class Strategies and the Education Market: The Middle Classes and Social Advantage*, RoutledgeFalmer.
- Livesey, C. and Lawson, T. (2005) *AS Sociology for AQA*, Hodder Arnold.
- Whitty, G. (2002) *Making Sense of Education Policy*, Paul Chapman Publishing.

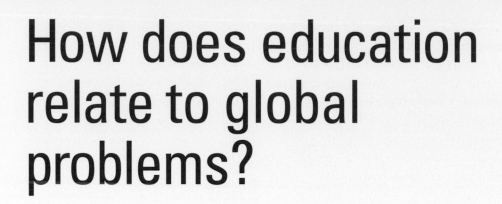

How does education relate to global problems?

Our focus so far has been principally on the British education system, sometimes reinforced by American research. In other parts of the world, many children do not attend school at all. If they do, they may have to leave before they learn the basics. Why is there such a disparity in educational provision around the world?

How many of the world's children cannot attend school?

According to Oxfam, there are 115 million children who have never attended school and a further 150 million who started school but dropped out before they could read and write. This means that about one third of the children in the developing world are not completing 4 years of basic education. One third of this out-of-school population live in sub-Saharan Africa, while in south Asia and Latin America millions of children are also denied education. As a result, one in four adults in the developing world is illiterate. Two thirds of these are women, because boys are often given priority when it comes to attending school.

Why is schooling essential?

You might assume that rural people who work on the land do not need an education, but basic literacy and numeracy are vital in order to participate in everyday life. The functional illiteracy that is widespread in much of the developing world means that millions of people cannot read well enough to understand healthcare leaflets, instructions on medicines and baby products, employment contracts and property deeds concerning who owns a piece of land. These individuals can easily be exploited by educated (and therefore more powerful) people, and their children may suffer through their ignorance of basic healthcare and hygiene. Oxfam has calculated that in Ghana, children of educated mothers are twice as likely to survive to their fifth birthday as those of uneducated mothers. In Pakistan, it has been claimed that providing an extra year of schooling for 1000 girls would prevent about 60 infant deaths. Literate mothers are more likely to immunise their children, take them to clinics for treatment and understand the causes and treatments of life-threatening conditions such as diarrhoea and respiratory infections.

Women tend to have more children in societies that have inadequate welfare systems, particularly in rural economies where many hands are needed to work the land or tend cattle. A lack of knowledge about contraception, another effect of illiteracy, is an additional reason for large families. It is ironic that these women, responsible for many young lives in particularly hazardous environments, are the least likely to be well enough educated to cope with the task, or to be able to teach their daughters how to read and the basics of healthcare.

Jennifer Wilson

School children in Malawi

It is rare for such communities to be able to fund free and easily accessible education. Such provisions as there are will be targeted predominantly at boys.

How do global inequalities affect education?

Although education was established as essential in the Universal Declaration of Human Rights (1948), global inequalities mean that many developing nations lack the resources to fund it adequately. International trade, skewed in favour of the industrialised north, continues to increase the gap between rich and poor countries, while many southern governments have been forced to reduce educational spending to pay debts on loans taken out many years ago. At the 1990 World Conference on Education for All, over 150 developing countries agreed to provide every child with primary education by the year 2000. Most of these countries have been forced to abandon their plans because they have received less international aid and debt relief than expected. Some countries, such as India, have, despite their conference resolutions, prioritised military spending over education.

Though a low national income often correlates with low expenditure on education, this is not always the case. The Oxfam Educational Performance Index (EPI) produces a value for each country, combining the enrolment rate, the completion rate and the ratio of female-to-male enrolment at primary school level. This can then be compared with the country's per capita income. Many countries in Latin America, the Middle East and sub-Saharan Africa have lower EPIs than they should have, according to their economies, while Cuba, Sri Lanka and China have achieved better access to education than might be expected. The varying social policies of different countries are important factors in determining how much is spent on education.

In Britain, it is only in the final stages of education that low family income may mean a student needs to drop out. In most developing countries, family poverty is the main reason for illiteracy. It costs more than a fifth of the average household income to send one child to school in many African countries. Parents often pay high fees for poor-quality education in overcrowded classrooms, sharing books and having to meet the costs of their own stationery. The dangers of having to walk five or more miles to school discourage parents from sending girls. In addition, children at school cannot contribute to the household income, which is a double disadvantage for families who need money for essential food or medicines.

Why is there 'gender apartheid' in education?

In many rural areas in the developing world, several hours of a woman's day are taken up with collecting water and firewood, pounding grains and tending the family plot. These are tasks in which young girls are often expected to help, meaning that, if there are scarce funds for education, boys are more likely than girls to be sent to school.

Traditional attitudes to female roles are another major reason for gender apartheid (treatment of girls as inferior). For example, when the Taliban government took power in Afghanistan, mixed schools were abolished and girls were sent home, with the excuse that separate schools for them would be built at a later date.

Oxfam argues that, if the initial cost can be met, educating children actually helps families out of poverty. It increases their earning potential, whether they work for others or learn to farm more effectively for themselves. As witnessed in Britain since the 1970s, improved education for girls increases their ambitions and encourages them to delay childbearing, thus reducing their family size. The life expectancy of literate women is longer and their skills benefit their communities. Many women become teachers and healthcare workers, or they organise other women in cooperatives.

How do Marxists view global educational inequalities?

Unfortunately, many families in the developing world have little control over the amount of money they earn, and thus how much they can invest in education. International factors, such as unfair trade, have a major impact, not only on the economies and welfare systems of developing countries, but also on the incomes of individual workers. The plummeting price of coffee in world markets means that many families in northern Tanzania now earn too little to send their children to school.

The Make Poverty History campaign in 2005 suggests that there is widespread popular concern about global inequalities, but many of the richest nations make overseas aid a relatively low priority. Oxfam estimates that for the cost of just one of the cruise missiles fired on Baghdad, about 100 schools could have been built in Africa. Less than 20% of the educational aid given by industrialised nations is for primary education, where it is needed the most. Far more money goes to higher education, producing small elites of government officials and industrialists while failing the needs of the majority.

Followers of Marxist dependency theory, such as B. Avalos ('Neocolonialism and education in Latin America', in K.Watson (ed) *Education in the Third World*, Croom Helm, 1982), argue that when developed nations intervene in the education programmes of poorer countries, they aim to reproduce the structure of industrialised capitalist societies. This is a form of cultural imperialism (a powerful country imposing its ideas on others), in which vocationally educated people are viewed as 'human capital', producers of industrial wealth through skilled work, with universal literacy being neglected. Modernisation theorists argue that such aid will improve the economies of emerging nations and that the wealth generated will trickle down to poorer citizens, but Marxists disagree with this claim.

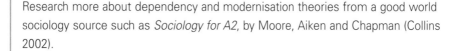

Task 7.1

Research more about dependency and modernisation theories from a good world sociology source such as *Sociology for A2*, by Moore, Aiken and Chapman (Collins 2002).

Avalos comments on the links between education and power. She notes that international aid agencies were reluctant to fund mass primary education in South America based on the methods of the educationalist Paulo Freire. His radical ideas, already mentioned in Chapter 1, were thought likely to encourage revolutionary activity in the poor. He was imprisoned for his views in 1964 and then spent 16 years in exile.

This example reminds us that educational content is as important as the amount of education received. Marxists argue that Western educational systems imposed on developing nations keep them in a state of dependency, failing to meet local needs. During colonial times, schools set up in Africa and India taught the English language and European religion and culture. Education in Spanish in Peru has alienated people from their indigenous culture. Though regimes have changed, elites educated in those systems have often resisted attempts to introduce mass education through local languages and cultures because of the threat to their own status. Yet there is clearly a need for each education system to reflect its national heritage rather than the values of dominant nations.

Many governments have recently encouraged local communities to build their own informal schools, particularly in rural areas, using local people to pass on their skills to others on a part-time basis. This might involve teaching literacy, numeracy and farming techniques. Ivan Illich (see page 20) would have applauded such schemes, which encourage people to take control of their own learning rather than depending on paid teachers. However, Webster (1990) suggests that it is a poor substitute for a formal education system and is unlikely to improve significantly the plight of millions of the world's poorest children.

Can education in Britain reduce global problems?

In order for developing nations to afford educational systems equal to those of the developed world, there needs to be a complete change in the international balance of power. To encourage more humane attitudes, many Western nations are changing what children learn, introducing into their curricula elements of development education, world studies or education for sustainability. You may have studied world sociology — the citizenship specification covers urgent issues such as global warming and other forms of environmental degradation. Though most children now have some grasp of such problems, only a minority of schools participate in practical projects, for example by becoming Eco-Schools (see Task 7.2).

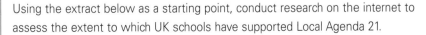

Task 7.2

Using the extract below as a starting point, conduct research on the internet to assess the extent to which UK schools have supported Local Agenda 21.

> Eco-Schools is a programme for environmental management and certification, and sustainable development education, for schools. Its holistic, participatory approach and combination of learning and action make it an ideal way for schools to embark on a meaningful path to improving the environments of schools and their local communities, and of influencing the lives of young people, school staff, families, local authorities, NGOs etc.
>
> (from www.eco-schools.org/aboutus/aboutus.htm)

Guidance

Look up the UK Youth Parliament, Defra, Friends of the Earth, WWF and Oxfam websites.

There have also been attempts to combat terrorism through schools. In September 2006, the Muslim Council of Britain launched Footsteps, a scheme intended to take speakers into schools to encourage Muslim students to pursue their studies, reducing alienation and disillusionment, and to change the opinions of non-Muslim students, who may hold Islamophobic views following the 7/7 London terrorist attacks and the alleged failed plot at Heathrow Airport. The founders of Footsteps believe it is essential to quell extremist ideologies in youngsters before they leave school.

The London pub bombings in 1999, which targeted homosexuals and ethnic minorities, and the recent growth in anti-Semitic attacks are reminders of other equality problems that education needs to embrace. Teaching needs to encourage empathy for all groups, environmental responsibility and global awareness. Whatever their league table position, institutions going some way towards achieving this can hardly be described as 'failing schools'.

Summary

- The lack of schooling in many parts of the developing world makes educational problems in the UK seem trivial in comparison.
- Causes of inadequate and inappropriate education include poverty, 'gender apartheid' and cultural imperialism.
- Improved education in the UK could enhance students' understanding of global and environmental problems and reduce inter-group conflict.

Research suggestion

If you have relatives or contacts who have lived abroad, you could conduct semi-structured interviews to gain insight into the educational systems they may have experienced.

Useful websites

- Oxfam education
  www.oxfam.org.uk/what_we_do/issues/education/index.htm
- Centre for Global Development — education download (American)
  www.cgdev.org/content/publications/detail/2844

Further reading

- Regan, C. (ed.) (2002) *80:20 Development in an Unequal World*, Teachers in Development Education.
- Watkins, K. (2000) *The Oxfam Education Report*, Oxfam.
- Webster, A. (1990) *Introduction to the Sociology of Development*, Palgrave.

Glossary

alienation
:   having no control over work conditions and no sense of fulfilment

anomie
:   a lack of shared values, accompanied by a feeling of moral confusion

banding
:   dividing children into general-ability groups, so that they study all or most subjects in that group

bourgeoisie
:   owners of the means of producing wealth, such as factories; also known as the ruling class or capitalists

city academies
:   secondary schools set up from 2002 to replace failing urban comprehensives

city technology colleges
:   schools set up in 1988 to emphasise IT and business links; sponsored by private companies

collective consciousness
:   the feeling of being bonded to society by sharing its distinctive cultural traditions and values

compensatory education
:   schemes aimed at improving the educational opportunities of disadvantaged groups by providing additional stimulation and resources

comprehensive schools
:   state secondary schools admitting students of all abilities

conflict perspective
:   Marxist focus on the potential for struggle between the proletariat asserting their rights and the bourgeoisie maintaining their power; or feminist or anti-racist focus on competing groups

consensus perspective
:   functionalist, control theory or New Right focus on the importance of shared values and keeping society orderly and united

cultural capital

the idea that accessing high culture depends on having financial capital; those at the top of the social ladder can afford to buy this sort of culture for their children, making educational success more likely

cultural deprivation

a controversial view that those at the bottom of the social structure lack the values and attitudes needed for educational success

cultural imperialism

a powerful country imposing its ideas on less powerful ones

cultural or new racism

a cluster of views about the abilities and attributes of ethnic groups, such as supposing that Afro-Caribbeans prefer macho street culture while Asians enjoy study

cultural reproduction

passing cultural knowledge and attitudes down the generations

culture of poverty

fatalistic attitude said to make the poor unable to take advantage of any opportunities that arise

cycle of poverty

material deprivation passed down the generations of a family

dependency theory

a view held by Marxists, among others, that developing nations contribute to the problems of developing countries by exploiting them

discrimination

acting on prejudices against or for members of a particular group: direct discrimination is deliberately different treatment of group members; indirect discrimination may involve treating everyone the same without realising that this creates special difficulties for members of some groups

education action zones

a government scheme from 1998 to raise standards in clusters of schools in disadvantaged areas through local initiatives

education priority areas

a government scheme in the 1960s that gave extra funding to some disadvantaged urban areas so that they could expand pre-school education, attract more teachers and equip schools better in order to improve literacy

egoism
pursuing one's own goals rather than the good of the group

elaborated code
according to Bernstein, middle-class speech patterns involving varied vocabulary and complex grammatical structure

embourgeoisement
people of working-class background adopting middle-class behaviour patterns

ethnic group
a group that sees itself as culturally distinct from other groupings in a society and is seen by others as distinctive; differences include country of origin, language, religion, dress or other aspects of culture

ethnocentric curriculum
a school syllabus that reflects the history and culture of the dominant group and ignores or marginalises the cultures of less influential ethnic groups

false consciousness
acceptance of inequalities as a result of capitalist socialisation

formula funding
schools receiving money according to the number of pupils on roll

functional illiteracy
inability to read well enough for everyday practicalities

gatekeeper
approachable member of a group used by sociologists to gain access to that group

gender apartheid
separate treatment of females as inferiors

heterogeneous
consisting of different kinds, such as people from many different backgrounds

hidden curriculum
the values transmitted unofficially in a school through the ways teachers treat different groups of students and staff, and the way it is organised

ideology
a set of biased beliefs, such as capitalist doctrine

independent schools
educational institutions that are not part of the state system; most of the students pay fees

institutional racism
the workings of organisations, rules and practices that have the effect of discriminating against particular ethnic groups

interactionists
sociologists whose methods involve closely studying the way people interpret each other's actions and react accordingly

labelling
stereotyping people such as school students, by basing judgements on inadequate evidence, often related to social characteristics

looking-glass self
a sense of identity reflecting other people's reactions to the individual concerned

machismo
aggressive, self-inflated masculinity

macrosociologists
sociologists interested in studying large social systems

marketisation
the way competition between schools has led to undue effort to secure a positive image and attract students through self-advertising

means of production
sources of wealth generation, such as factories, industrial plants and land

meritocracy
a system in which those who develop their skills and work hard are rewarded accordingly, regardless of social background

microsociologists
sociologists interested in how people interact in small groups, such as in classrooms

modernisation theory
belief that traditional societies will benefit from the influence of developed nations

national curriculum
subjects that students in state schools all over the country have to study

official curriculum
subjects taught in school

open enrolment
a system whereby students can apply to any non-selective state school that has places

positional theory
Boudon's idea that people often prefer to remain at the same social level as their parents (social reproduction)

prejudice
learned beliefs and values leading to bias for, or against, members of particular groups

progressive education
child-centred methods of teaching and learning, favoured by liberals and disliked by traditionalists

proletariat
the working mass of the population; wage labourers

reserve army of labour
unemployed people, usually desperate enough to accept low wages; a reminder to those in work that, if they demand better conditions, they can easily be replaced

restricted code
according to Bernstein, working-class language with limited vocabulary, disjointed sentence structure and a lack of explanation

role allocation
selecting people for jobs at different levels in society, usually according to qualifications gained

selective schools
schools that choose students according to measured ability

self-fulfilling prophecy
predictions about an outcome, such as a student's academic attainment, with those involved acting upon them in such a way that they come true

social reproduction
family members remaining at a similar level on the social scale down the generations

social solidarity
a feeling of identification with the group and the sense that more can be achieved by acting together

sponsored mobility

identifying people for social advancement at an early age and supporting them as they prepare for their rise to the top

streaming

dividing children into ability groups for the teaching of a specific subject according to their aptitude for that subject; also known as setting

structuralists

sociologists who view aspects of social life such as education in terms of how they affect institutions and large groups in society

tripartite system

the three types of secondary school established in 1944; students were selected according to their performance in the 11-plus examination

trust schools

state schools with control over their own curriculum and admissions; proposed by a government White Paper in 2005

typing

stereotyping or labelling people

value consensus

fundamental moral beliefs shared by members of a society

vocational education

work-related courses and experiences organised by schools